THE FUTURE ENTREPRENEUR

Start Your Own Business Today

KINGSTONE P. NGWIRA

authorHOUSE®

AuthorHouse™
1663 Liberty Drive
Bloomington, IN 47403
www.authorhouse.com
Phone: 833-262-8899

Published by AuthorHouse 10/02/2020

ISBN: 978-1-6655-0231-3 (sc)
ISBN: 978-1-6655-0229-0 (hc)
ISBN: 978-1-6655-0230-6 (e)

Library of Congress Control Number: 2020919002

Print information available on the last page.

Contents

Dedication

To the millions who have not started their own businesses

To all who have believed in my vision.

To my executive leadership team at Great Dominion Holdings Limited (GDHL). Thank you for your visionary support.

To my beloved wife Shannila, sons, Pastor Prince and Gift, you are my greatest inspiration to achieve my strategic vision. Thank you for supporting and comforting me during challenging times.

Acknowledgements

This work is a function of a life time of learning and experience obtained from starting different business ventures over the years.

Writing a book is a daunting task. This book has taken more than four (4) years of preparation and has been written in (2) two years. Hence the obvious impact that it will bring upon your life as a reader.

To my son, Pastor Prince, for your unwavering support.

To the Board of Directors of Great Dominion Holdings Limited (GDHL) in Lilongwe, Malawi. You are part of my history.

Preface

If only you can focus on implementing what you will learn from this book in the next 60 days, I can guarantee you that you will be on the path to start your own business. Your success is not dependent on climate of your country.

The book presents entrepreneurial skills which if applied will guarantee one's great business start up. Prof. Kingstone Prince Ngwira delivers to you in this book proven principles and concepts on how you can start your own business. It is envisaged that anyone that reads this book and take the steps of applying the skills which have been highlighted will emerge a champion in starting his or her own business.

Entrepreneurship represents a vital source of change in all facets of society, empowering individuals to seek opportunities where others see insurmountable problems. Technologicaly entrepreneurship as a style of business leadership involves identifying highly-potential, technology-intensive commercial opportunities, gathering resources such as talent and capital, and managing rapid growth and significant risks using principled decision-making skills.

Early in my career, it became obvious to me that education gives you a big edge in business. Risk, which is always a part of doing business, is substantially reduced when you learn everything about what you are getting into. People who are more educated and have prepared even beyond formal education have an entrepreneurship advantage. That is what has greatly contributed to my success.

The purpose of this book is targeting those that aspire to start their own business ventures and University students pursuing entrepreneurial or business courses who have a vision to establish their own business venture. I have the overwhelming confidence and beliefs that such group of people will get something from this book. I also believe that anyone who has a failed business venture will read this book and learn the secrets which will help avoid pitfalls in future.

By learning from the successful entrepreneurs in this book, you are way ahead of the game. This is why this book is a must read book for you which will help you to realize your dream in life.

Kingstone P. Ngwira

Introduction

The world economies are in tatters, therefore your job is in trouble or indeed making it difficult for you to get a job if you do not have one. In one of my books entitled, "Secrets of Successful Wealthy Entrepreneurs" I said, "I wished I knew then what I know now." It goes without saying that if you do what successful people do, there is a high probability that you can also become successful. This is the reason why I want to thank you for deciding to read this book because whenever the principles and concepts presented in this book will be applied, you will be able to start your own business anywhere in the world.

This book is written from three sources: first, accessed knowledge from my mentors on entrepreneurship; second, are courses which I have taught in Universities both local and international as a Professor of Business and Management Studies, and above all, my own entrepreneurial experience in my own entrepreneurial ventures.

I would like to emphasize the purpose of this book with joy that while this book is going to empower would-be Entrepreneurs to start their new business ventures it is not only for them. The book is also for those that are already in business but are struggling.

PART ONE

THE BUSINESS OF THE 21ST CENTURY

CHAPTER 1

Developing the Strategic Vision

We live in troubled times. The years we are in have brought a steady parade of fear and panic in our everyday life. Many business ventures today are facing difficulties such as corporate decline, risking closure, and bankruptcy and even winding up in some instances. This results in companies not to think of hiring more staff and the common practice is that employees are retrenched, downsized and organizational layers delayered. This is a call to start your own business and develop your Strategic Vision.

What is a Strategic Vision?

Strategic Vision is a description of the Road Map which answers three key questions: Where are we? Where do we want to be? And how do we get there? Therefore the management's views and conclusions about the organization's long term direction is what constitute a strategic vision.

There is no escaping the need for a strategic vision. Armed with a clear well conceived business course for the organization to follow, managers have a beacon to guide resource allocation and a basis for crafting a strategy to get the company where it needs to go.

Companies whose mangers neglect the task of thinking strategically about the company's future business path are prone to drift aimlessly and lose any claim to being an industry leader

Business Mission Statement

A company's mission statement is typically focused on its present business scope: "who we are and what we do." Mission Statements broadly describe an organization's present capabilities, customer focus, activities and business make up

The difference between strategic vision and mission statement is that a mission statement speaks to what a company is doing today while strategic vision generally has much greater direction – setting and strategy – making value. Mission Statement has two questions: In what business are we in? and why are we in business.

Setting the Strategic Objectives

This involves converting the strategic vision into specific performance outcomes for the company to achieve. The purpose of setting objectives is to convert managerial statements of strategic vision and business mission into Setting Objectives and then measuring whether they are achieved or not help managers track an organization's progress.

Managers of the best performing companies tend to set objectives that require stretch and disciplined effort. The challenge of trying to achieve bold, aggressive performance targets pushes an organization to be more inventive, to exhibit some urgency in improving both its financial performance (financial objectives) and business position (strategic objectives(and to be more intentional and focused in its actions, specific performance targets – results and outcomes the organization wants to achieve.

Strategy Formulation

The challenge of strategic vision is to be able to understand complex issues facing organizations and develop long term organizational success. Strategy formulation requires understanding of the term strategy.

You can take a characteristics approach in order to define what this is. A strategy is usually concerned with long term direction of an organization. Strategic decisions are likely to be concerned with the scope of organization (s) activities eg. what should the organization's core business be for instance. Here scope of work becomes very fundamental to the strategy. This is because it concerns the way in which those responsible as managers conceive the organization's boundaries.

Strategic decisions aim at achieving some advantage for the organization over competition. Strategy can be seen as a search for strategic fit with the business environment. This could mean major resource shifts or changes in an organization e.g. decision to reposition one in the market.

Strategy also creates opportunities by building on an organization's resources and competences. This is called the resource based view of strategy.

Strategy and Strategic Decisions

Strategy is the direction and scope of an organization over the long term which achieves advantage in a changing environment through its configuration of resources and competences with the objective of fulfilling stakeholder expectations.

Thomson and Strickland (2007) points out that a company's strategy is the game plan management is using to stake out a market position, conduct its operations, attract and please customers.

In crafting a strategy management is saying, in effect "among all the paths and actions we could have chosen, we have decided to move in this direction, focus on these markets and customer needs, compete in this fashion, allocate our resources and energies in these ways and rely on these particular approaches to doing business."

A strategy thus entails managerial choices among alternatives and signals organizational commitment to specific markets, competitive approaches and ways of operating. Closely related to the concept of strategy is the concept of a company's business model. This is a term now widely applied to management's plan for making money in a particular business. More formally, a company's business model deals with the revenue cost-profit economics of its strategy.

Building on resources and competences (capability) require values and expectations of different stakeholders. Thus they are likely to be complex in nature in many cases made under conditions of uncertainty.

Levels of Strategy

Strategies exist at a number of levels in an organization. We distinguish three levels of strategy

1. Corporate Strategy Level

This is concerned with overall purpose and scope of an organization and how value will be added to the different parts (business units) of the organization. This could include issues of geographical coverage such as: diversity of products; service or business units; resource allocation between different parts of the organization.

2. Business Level Strategy

Corporate strategy is also likely to be concerned with the expectations of owners the shareholders and the stock market. It may take form in an explicit or implicit way which reflects expectations. Business level strategy is about how to compete successfully in particular markets.

This concerns which products or services should be developed in which markets. How can advantage over competitors be achieved in order to achieve organization goals and objectives. It could also be long term profitability or market share growth.

Whereas corporate strategy level involves decisions about organization as a whole strategic decisions here need to be related to strategic business units. A strategic business unit (SBU) is part of an organization for which there is a distinct external market for goods or services that is different from another SBU.

These can be conceptualized in geographical terms, structured around regional business units, hence they become the primary foci for business level strategy. These would change with the change in the scope and type of customers and products.

There should clearly be a link between SBU level strategy and corporate level strategies that both assist and constrain these business level strategies. In the case of Dell, product level and internet were dictated centrally. Marketing and customer support was regionalized.

In public sector, a SBU might be a part of the organization or service for which there is a distinct client group. It is important to remember that a SBU is a unit of organization for strategy making purposes. It may or may not be a structural part of the organization such as a department or a division.

3. Operational Strategy

This can be described as the third level strategy. These are strategies concerned with how the component parts of an organization deliver effectively the corporate and business level strategies in terms of processes and people. In most businesses successful businesses depend to a large extent on decisions that are taken on activities that occur at the operational level. The integration of operational decisions and strategy is therefore of great importance as mentioned earlier.

Strategic Position

Understanding the strategic position is concerned with identifying the impact on strategy of the external environment an organization's strategic capability resources and competencies) and the expectations and influence of stakeholders.

The organization exists in the context of a complex political social technological environment. The environment could be dynamic and sometimes more complex in other organizations than others. These challenges lead to opportunities and threats on the business.

Strategic Capability

This is made up of resources and competencies. You can think about this by considering strengths and weaknesses (whether its is a competitive advantage /disadvantage). The aim is to form a view of the internal influences and constraints on strategic choices for the future.

It is usually what we call core competencies, a combination of resources and high levels of competence that provide advantages **which competitors find difficult to imitate.**

Strategic Position

Influences of expectations on an organization's purposes are crucial in strategic positioning important. For instance who should the organization serve/ how should managers be held responsible.

Note that the expectations of various stakeholders also affect purposes. Who prevails depends on who has the greatest power. Cultural influences from within the organization and around the world also influence the strategy and organization follows.

Strategic Choices

Involves understanding the underlying bases for future strategy at both the business and corporate levels and the options for developing strategy in both the directions in which strategy might move and methods of development

There are strategic choices in terms of how the organization seeks to compete at business level. This involves the identification of a basis for competitive advantage. This arises from an understanding of the markets, customers and strategic capability of the organization.

At the highest level there are issues of corporate level strategy. These are concerned with the scope of an organization's strategies. It includes decisions about portfolio of products and or business and spread of markets.

For most organizations international strategy are a key a part of corporate level strategy. Parenting is part of this strategy. It involves the relationship between separate parts of the business and how the corporate parent adds value to these parts e.g. exploring synergies within an organization can add value.

Strategy into position

Translating strategy into action is concerned with ensuring that strategies are working in practice. Structuring an organization to support performance includes organizational structures, processes and relationships and the interaction between these enabling success through the way in which separate resources of an organization support strategies.

Managing strategy involves change most often. How the context of an organization should influence the approach to change. Different types of roles for people managing change.

Strategy Development Process

These refer to the ways in which strategy develops in businesses. It considers different explanations of how strategies develop within the strategic context in businesses. These processes can be grouped into two main types.

Strategy development as deliberate management intent This is the concept of intended strategies. Second are explanations that place more emphasis on the emergency of strategy to develop through a complex combination of these various processes.

CHAPTER 2

The 21ˢᵗ Century Entrepreneur

The pace and magnitude of change will continue to accelerate in the new millennium. Having the evolution and transformation of entrepreneurial firms match this pace will be critical. Building dynamic capabilities that are differentiated from those of the emerging competitors is the major challenge for growing firms that seek to adapt to the changing landscape.

Two ways of building dynamic capabilities are internal – utilization of the creativity and knowledge from employees. And external – the search for external competencies to complement the firm's existing capabilities. This calls for a business to be an adaptive firm. Adaptive firm is a firm that increases opportunities, initiates change and instills desire to be innovative.

What is entrepreneurship?

An entrepreneur is one who creates a new business in the face of risk and uncertainty for the purpose of achieving profit and growth by identifying opportunities and assembling the necessary resources to capitalize on those opportunities. Entrepreneurs usually start with nothing more than an idea – often a simple one – and then organize the resources necessary to transform that idea into a sustainable business.

One business writer says an entrepreneur is "someone who takes nothing for granted, assumes change is possible and follows through someone incapable of confronting reality without thinking about ways to improve it and for whom action is a natural consequence of thought.

Many people dream of owning their businesses and become wealth but most of them never launch the business or company. Those who take an entrepreneurial plunge however will experience the thrill of creating something grand from nothing; they will also discover the challenges and difficulties of building a business "from scratch". Whatever their reasons for choosing entrepreneurship many organize that true satisfaction comes only from running their own businesses the way they choose.

Researchers have invested a great deal of time and effort over the last decade studying these entrepreneurs and trying to paint a clear picture of the "entrepreneurial personality." Although these studies have produced several characteristics entrepreneurs tend to exhibit, none of them has isolated a set of traits required for success.

The brief summary of entrepreneurial profile includes but not limited to: desire for responsibility, preference for moderate risk, confidence in their ability to succeed, desire for immediate feedback, high level of energy, future orientation, skill at organizing, value of achievement over money, high degree of commitment, tolerance of ambiguity, flexibility and tenacity.

The entrepreneur

The word entrepreneur is derived from the French word "entreprendre" meaning to "undertake." Entrepreneurship is a way of thinking, reasoning and acting that is opportunity obsessed, holistic in approach and leadership balanced.

Entrepreneurship results in creation enhancement, realization and renewal of value, not just for owners, but for all participants and stakeholders. On the other hand we have intrapreneurs. These are managers that are employed in an organization but using entrepreneurial skills.

Entrepreneurs are supposed to drive a revolution that is transforming and renewing economics worldwide. Entrepreneurship is the essence of free enterprise because the birth of new businesses gives a market economy its vitality.

Entrepreneurs have many of the same character traits as leaders. Similarly to the early great man theories of leadership; however trait based theories of entrepreneurship are increasingly being called into question. Entrepreneurs are often constructed with managers and administrators who said to be more methodical and less prone to risk- talking.

Such person centric models of entrepreneurship have shown questionable validity not least as many real life entrepreneurs operate in teams rather than as single individuals. Still, a vast but now clearly dated literature studying the entrepreneurial personality found that certain traits seem to be associated with entrepreneurs.

Types of Entrepreneurs

There are four types of entrepreneurs: innovators, the calculating inventor, the over optimistic promoter, and the organization builder. These types are not related to the personality but to the type of opportunity the entrepreneur faces.

The entrepreneur to succeed he or she needs to process the following charactering: the entrepreneur should have an enthusiastic vision, the driving force of an enterprise; the entrepreneur's vision is usually supported by an interlocked collection of specific ideas not available to the market place; the overall blue print to realize the vision is clear, however details may be incomplete, flexible and involving, entrepreneur promotes the vision with enthusiastic passion; with persistence and determination, the entrepreneur develops strategies to change the vision into reality; the entrepreneur takes the initial responsibility to cause a vision to become a success; entrepreneurs take prudent risks.

They asses cost, market/ customer needs and persuade others to join and help; and an entrepreneur is usually a positive thinker and decision maker.

The Entrepreneurial Age

The 21st century is perceived to be an entrepreneur age. Entrepreneur is often perceived as a difficult undertaking, as a vast majority of new business fails. Entrepreneurial activities are substantially different depending on the type of organization that is being started. Entrepreneurship ranges in scale from solo projects also known as swivivalsts (individualism) to major undertaking many job opportunities.

Entrepreneurship is the sense of free enterprise because the birth of new business gives a market economy its vitality. Many business commentators say that the one extreme an entrepreneur is a person of every high aptitude who pioneers change, processing characteristics found in only a very small fraction of the population. On the other hand extreme of definitions, anyone wants to work for he/she is considered to be an entrepreneur.

Peters (2012) supports the above views and states that entrepreneurship results in creation, enhancement, realization of value, not just for owners, for all participants and stakeholders. At the heart of this process is the creation and or recognition of opportunities followed by the will and initiative to seize these opportunities. Thus it requires willingness to take risks, both personal and financial- but in a very calculated fashion in order to constantly shift the odds to your favorable balancing the risks with potential reward.

Many writers share above views and comment that entrepreneurs devise ingenious strategies to marshal their limited resources. This means that they are people who see opportunities where others see chaos. They move into an area and start making money while others wonder-what are these people doing on this dead place.

CHAPTER 3

Deciding a Business Venture

Buying a Franchise and Other Businesses

Buying a franchise and other businesses is one of the best ways to start a new business, if you do it right, is to buy a franchise or other established business. While people typically think of Mc- Donald's, KFC, Dunkin' Donuts, or Baskin Robbins when they think of franchises, the fact is that franchises come in almost every industry.

The same is true for an already established business. They can be found for sale in every industry and take a lot of the risk out of the entrepreneurship equation. Franchising is a method of distributing services or products. With a franchise system, the franchisor (the company selling the franchise) offers its trademark and business system to the buyer, or franchisee who pays a fee for the right to do business under the franchisor's name using the franchisor's methods.

The franchisee is given instructions on how to run the business as the franchisor does using the franchisor's name and the franchisor supports the franchisee with expertise, training, advertising, and a proven system. Buying into a proven system is important. The franchises that work best are those where the franchisor has worked out the kinks and translated its business into a systematic procedure that the franchisee follows.

Do what the franchisor did, and you should get the results that it got; that's the idea. As franchisors are wont to say, when ability to publicize it properly and work cooperatively with the media can become one of the stories if you do it right. So just how do you get the press to pay attention to your business? Begin by reading the paper or watching your local news closely and noticing which reporters do stories about small businesses.

Successful franchisors have certain traits in common. Following are the traits that are most important. If you can find a franchisor that has these traits, you are headed in the right direction.

The Franchisor supports the franchisees

The best franchises are ones where the franchisor sees its relationship with the franchisees as a partnership. As Steve Reinemund, the former head of Pizza Hut, puts it, "Franchisees are only as successful as the parent company and the parent company is only as successful as the franchisees."

Not only do such exceptional franchisors offer plenty of communication, opportunities for growth within the company, and help during hard times, they also offer lots of advice and training. A good example of this is Dunkin' Donuts. To support new franchisees, it created Dunkin' Donuts University.

There, franchisees and their personnel are invited to attend a six-week success program that teaches them everything from basic instructions on how to run the business to how to produce the products, deal with employees, and use equipment. It even offers advice on inventory control and accounting. Now that's support.

The Franchisor Is Committed To Customer Service

The great franchisors don't just give lip service to customer service, they teach it to everyone in the organization, and live it on a daily basis. That's critical, because if people are treated well at other outlets, that, in turn, gives your individual franchise a good name too. As the Pizza Hut chairman put it, "We are committed to more than just good service, we are committed to providing legendary service." you buy a franchise, you are in business for yourself but not by yourself.

The reason that a franchise can be a smart business decision is that in the right franchise system, the franchisor has already made the mistakes so you don't have to. Franchising should reduce your risk. You need not reinvent the wheel. In exchange for its expertise, training, and help, however, you will be required to give up some independence and do things the franchisor's way. Finding the right franchise With so many franchise systems from which to choose, the options can be dizzying.

Start Up Business Opportunity

Starting a successful business requires preparation, special talents, skills, competencies and abilities, leadership skills as well as resources. These are critical requirements before you step into any business. Experience and observation has shown that many businesses both great and small fail because of poor or lack of preparation. You need to know that Prior Proper Preparation Prevents Poor Performance. So I would like to say congratulations! The decision to start your own business can be one of the best you will ever make in your life. Owning your own business should be an exhilarating, inspiring, grand adventure; one full of new sights and experiences, delicious highs and occasional lows, tricky paths and, hopefully, big open sky's.

But to ensure that your business journey will be a fruitful one, it is important to understand all that becoming an entrepreneur entails. first thing to understand is that there are tradeoffs when you decide to start a business. Difficult bosses, annoying coworkers, peculiar policies, demands upon your time, and limits on how much money you can make are traded for independence, creativity, opportunity, and power.

Setting up new business collides with the wishes of established competitors, who want all the customers' income they can get. Many people start their business adventure dreaming of riches and freedom.

But by the same token, you also swap a regular paycheck and benefits for no paycheck and no benefits. A life of security, comfort, and regularity is traded for one of uncertainty.

Start – up influences

Why does anybody want to take the risk of starting up their own business? It is hard work without guaranteed results. But millions do so every year around the world. The start-up is the bedrock of modern – day commercial wealth, the foundation of free-market economics upon which competition is based. So can economists shade light on the process?

Economists would tell us that new entrants into an industry can be expected when there is a rise in expected post-entry profitability for them. In other words, new entrants expect to make extra profits. Economists tell us that the rate of entry is related to the growth of the industry. They also tell us the entry is deterred by barriers such as high capital requirements, the existence of economies of scale, product differentiation restricted access to necessary in puts and so on.

What is more the rate of entry is lower in industries with high degrees of concentration where it may be assumed that firms combine to deter entry. However, research also tells us that whereas the rate of small firm start-up in these concentrated industries is lower, the rate of start-up for large firms is higher.

These seem useful, but perhaps obvious statements about start-ups, really happen and why? Somehow economists fail to explain convincingly the rationale for, and the process of, start-up. They seem to assume that there is a continuous flow of entrants into an industry just waiting for the possibility of extra profits. But people are not like that. They need to earn money to live; they have families who depend on them.

Benefits of Owning Your Own Business or Company

Surveys show that owners of businesses or companies believe they work harder, earn more money and are happier than if they worked for someone or for a corporation. Before launching any business venture every potential entrepreneur should consider the benefits and opportunities of business ownership.

Finding Sponsorship

A safer bet as an entry wedge may be to take advantage of the willingness of someone to help sponsor the startup in some manner. Typically the sponsor is a customer, a supplier or an investor in the startup venture. A prime requisite for all these types of sponsorship is that the sponsor as credible and likely to succeed regard entrepreneur and the venture. The strongest basis for this is usually a track record of prior accomplishment and a demonstration that the entrepreneur possesses the capacity to perform the critical tasks of the venture.

Acquiring a Going Concern

The final main entry strategy is to acquire a going concern. This can simplify the process of getting into business. A business can be viewed as basically a bundle of habits - customers buying, suppliers supplying, employees doing their jobs. In a going concern, those habits are already present.

Expertise in a going concern should already be present in employees of the business. Even if it is not, the buying entrepreneur should be able to obtain education and operating help from the selling owner to fill in the expertise needed. Consequently, it is fairly common to find businesses owned by entrepreneurs who bought them with no prior experience in that particular line of business and nevertheless succeeded.

Developing a New Product or Service Opportunity

What it takes to start a company around a new product or service includes, most importantly, the discovery of an intersection between the market for that product or service and away to create one.

Creating Parallel Competition by Developing a New Product or Service

Parallel competition is often fierce. By definition it involves firms that lack strong differentiation and therefore tend to compete on price, which drives margins down. The toughness of such competition will likely force the entrepreneur to be good at performing the functions of the business.

CHAPTER 4

The Mindset of an Entrepreneur

What is an entrepreneurial mindset?

Entrepreneurial mindset: a way of thinking that enables you to overcome challenges, be decisive, and accept responsibility for your outcomes. It is a constant need to improve your skills, learn from your mistakes, and take continuous action on your ideas. Anyone willing to do the work can develop an entrepreneurial mindset.

How to develop an entrepreneurial mindset

Anyone can learn how to act like an entrepreneur, build the habits, and learn some business hacks to fearlessly create a business or start a side hustle. You can work towards starting a business and earning passive income without quitting your job, without knowing how to code, and without a million-dollar idea. Having a proven online business model helps, too.

The Entrepreneurial Mindset Model

It is important that the entrepreneur maintains an entrepreneurial frame of mind. Figure 4.1 below illustrates the danger of entrepreneurs evolving into bureaucrats who in turn stifle innovation.

Fig. 4.1: Entrepreneurial Mindset Model

Future Goals

	Change	Status Quo
Perceived Capacity	Entrepreneur	Satisfied Manager
	Frustrated Manager	Classic Bureacrat

Source: Author (2020)

It has been noted that in some cases, success affects an entrepreneur's willingness to change and innovate. This is particularly true when the enterprise has developed a sense of complacency and when the entrepreneur likes this environment. The person does not want to change.

In fact, some entrepreneurs will create a bureaucratic environment where orders are issued from the top down and change initiated at the lower levels is not tolerated. As a result no one in the venture is willing (or encouraged) to become innovative or entrepreneurial because the owner – founder stifles such activity.

One study found that the entrepreneur directly affects the firm's growth orientation as measured by productivity goals, product market goals, hman resources goals and flexibility goals. If the entrepreneur hopes to maintain the creative climate that helped launch the venture in the first place, specific steps or measure must be taken.

The Adaptive Firm

It is important for entrepreneurs to establish a business that remains flexible beyond start up. Figure 4.2 below illustrates the concept of an adaptive firm.

Fig 4.2: Building the Adaptive Firm

Share the entrepreneur's vision	Institutionalized change as the venture's goal
Increase the perception of opportunity	Instill the desire to be innovative

Source: Routamaa (1999:20) International Small Business Journal

It is noted that the adaptive firm increases opportunity for its employees, initiates change and instills a desire to be innovative. Many business commentators say that entrepreneurs can build an adaptive firm by sharing the entrepreneurs's vision, increasing the perception of opportunity, institutualizing change as the venture's goal and instilling the desire to be innovative.

Learn to master your inner game

Most people are **afraid to start** pursuing their dreams. Or if they do start, they turn back at the first signs of struggle, convinced they don't have what it takes. This is why your thinking is so important to get right in the beginning. Being an entrepreneur starts with **that feeling inside you** – that entrepreneurial spirit you need to nourish and hone.

Whether you are an employee looking to level up your career, a worker exploring how to become a free lancer, or become a founder and CEO of your own company– when you master the entrepreneur mindset, you will begin to accomplish more goals than you ever imagined.

Here are the five characteristics of entrepreneurship:

1. Decisiveness

To succeed as an entrepreneur, you must gain the ability to look at a problem or situation, digest all available data (at that point in time), and make a confident decision to move forward. Your ability as a decision-maker will **make or break** your future successes. In fact, at the opposite end, indecision is one of the greatest causes of business failure. When you can't decide what to do, you delay taking action. In other words, you do nothing.

Think about how many dreams (and businesses) **failing to take action** has killed. Like many other skills an entrepreneur needs, being decisive is a skill that can (and should) be practiced and strengthened in your day to day life — starting with the tiniest decisions.

2. Confidence

There are many skills you will need to learn to accomplish everything you want in life. But how do you act confidently when you **don't know what you are doing?** You learn to act with confidence, the second characteristic of the entrepreneurial mindset. And one of the most important qualities of an entrepreneur is essential that you get used to the uncomfortable feeling of knowing that you don't know what you're doing.

Whether it's getting on stage to speak, launching your product, or learning how to start a blog and publishing your ideas to the world, we tend to see others doing it and incorrectly assume they've always been good at it.

They weren't born knowing how to speak confidently, launch successful products, or write excellent books. They also weren't born knowing how to become entrepreneurs.

They learned and we can, too.

The difference between appearing good or bad at something is often a matter of acting confidently.

The entrepreneurial mindset in action: Pretend you know what you're doing.

For example, here's how to become more confident, right now …

Looking confident, practiced, and skilled is what we admire in others. But looking confident and being confident are **two different things**.

Acting confident while getting on stage to give a speech to a packed room, even when your hands are violently shaking, is essential to learn the art of public speaking.

This works with everything. Here's what I mean.

Do you want to be a podcaster? Start podcasting.

Do you want to become a professional chef? Start cooking.

Do you want to be a copywriter? Start writing sales pages that convert.

Do you have side hustle ideas you want to start? Stop watching Netflix every night.

Do you want to learn email marketing? Start building your email list today.

Pretending you are good at something will enable you to do it confidently enough times until **you become good at it**.

The more you do this, the better you will become. It's counterintuitive, but it works every time. And if you aren't quite ready to take this leap, here are some motivational quotes to kick you in the ass.

3. Accountability

The entrepreneurial mindset comes from taking responsibility for your actions and outcomes.

You need to internalize and accept that:

- Everything that happens at work – YOU are responsible for.
- Everything that happens to your business – YOU are responsible for.
- Whether you succeed or fail, it is YOUR responsibility.

From this moment forward, you must accept responsibility for everything in your life and **hold yourself accountable** to it. Sorry to tell you, but nobody cares how little time, money, or external support you have to accomplish your goals. Your circumstances may not be your fault, but they are your responsibility.

All that matters is what you are doing RIGHT NOW to find your success. There are **no more excuses**. Accountability is required of entrepreneurs as well as successful employees. Stop passing the buck and blaming others.

Hold yourself accountable – even when you aren't to blame – and take action to fix the problem. The entrepreneurial mindset requires you to take complete control and hold yourself accountable to your outcomes – both good and bad. As James Altucher said on the podcast, life is a sentence of failures punctuated with brief successes.

4. Resilience

As an entrepreneur, you will need to learn to deal with making mistakes and failing. They are inevitable and a part of your growth. If every misstep plummets you into self-doubt, you have to change the way you look at being wrong.

This **mindset shift** takes resilience and is foundational to the entrepreneurial mindset. Success rarely happens in a straight line. Taking wrong turns and making mistakes is something that happens to everyone.

"The only people who don't make mistakes are the ones who don't do anything."

Resilience isn't only helpful when dealing with catastrophic mistakes. It's a way to handle the small, simple decisions you've made that didn't turn out right. Resilience enables you to think, act, and move iteratively — making small, incremental corrections along the way.

5. Humility

Humility is freedom from pride or arrogance, and it ties all of the characteristics of entrepreneurship. From decisiveness to confidence, humility will keep you **focused and centered**. From accountability to resilience, you will continue to move forward through failure, mistakes, and upsets.

This is accomplished with humility.

> *"If you are the smartest person in the room, you are in the wrong room."*
>
> — *Someone smarter than me.*

Along with humility comes coachability — the ability to be coached.

If you want to accomplish big things in life, you need to be **willing to learn from others** and nourish a growth mindset. To do big things, you need to grow. To grow, you need to learn. No matter what you are trying to accomplish, someone already has done it before you.

Thinking like an entrepreneur means seeking out mentors and coaches who have been where you are trying to go — and having the humility to accept their guidance. **Take the next step towards developing your**

entrepreneurial mindset. There are so many misconceptions around entrepreneurship and starting a business, it's no wonder there is so much doubt (and so little confidence).

A few common misconceptions that need to be dispelled are:

- Entrepreneurs are **born hustlers**
- You need a unique (and revolutionary) idea to be successful
- Starting an online business requires technical skills
- You can't succeed without **full-time effort**

To be clear, mastering your entrepreneurial mindset is not easy. Nobody said it was. The most important thing is to start by following **a proven formula**. You need to go into this journey knowing you can get past any obstacle that comes up — because you can and will.

PART TWO

HOW TO START BUSINESS OPERATIONS

CHAPTER 5

Getting the Basics Right

Preparation

In Ecclesiastes 3, we are told that there is a time for everything. You have to ask God "when" for your assignment. God knows the perfect time for you to set out. Moses in the book of Exodus struck for 40 years earlier than God's time. This sent him on personal exile, he was downgraded. Jesus, the son of God, was the natural son of Joseph for 30 years, until He became into the fullness of time.

For which of you intending to build a tower sitteth not down first and counteth the cost whether he have sufficient to finish it. Luke 14:28 Lest haply after he hath laid the foundation and is not able to finish it all that behold it begin to mock him saying this man began to build and was not able to finish. Luke 14:29-30 During the preparation time is when you need to set goals and proper planning in terms of required resources and sett.

Become a Great Leader

Starting or growing a successful great business requires you to become a great leader. Your personal leadership ability is the major limit on what you can achieve. Leadership is the major factor for business success. Leadership is the ability to get results through influence and this requires having a clear vision of the future of your great business and taking courage to take action with no guarantee success. Responsibilities of leadership include setting and achieving business goals, market and innovate – continuously seek faster, better, cheaper, easier ways to create and keep customers, set priorities and work on key tasks while supervising results. Additionally, leadership also involves solving problems, making decisions, leading by example, perform and get results.

Effective Management of Resources

To run a successful great business requires effective management of a variety of resources such as great people, equipment, property, cash, great brand, great product or service and inventory. Of all these resources cash is probably the most important. With sufficient cash a business has the ability to buy any of the other resources in which it may be deficient. Whether the purchase of that resource is worthwhile at the price required is another matter, but the purchase can still be made.

All the resources other than cash have a value to a business that is dependent on their availability, utilization, market demand and prevailing economic climate. It is cash and only cash that maintains a constant value and can easily be turned into other assets or resources.

Confirmation

This is seeking the affirmation of others in deciding what steps to take in starting your great business. God is never ting priorities. There is what is called "the fullness of time". It is the right time to step out into your God given assignment after a good preparation. You need to be sensitive to the right time, in order to make healthy progress. So prepare before stepping out into your great business and you will succeed.

Ambition

This is one's expectation or what one looks forward to achieving. Thus, it is a self – made plan. Nothing is practicing wrong with good ambitious. But, "without vision the people perish." Ambition is therefore liable to failure and can even destroy the ambitious one. Only the ambition that falls in line with God's drawn-out plan becomes fruitful and successful. Absalom was ambitious and his ambition killed him!

Dr. David Oyedepo says "ambition says, I want it by all means", but vision says, "I have it because God says it, and I am in His plan." Ambition is the brother of anxiety, whereas vision is a relative of peace.

Talents, Skills and Competencies

Special talents, skills, competencies and abilities are required for you to achieve your goal, impressions and ambitions of owning or running a successful great business. This is a call to clarify them and craft superior strategies to multiply and maximize them. When clarifying them you need to develop absolute clarity about who you are, what you want and the best way to achieve it. This leads to multiplication of your talents, skills, competences and abilities from which you leverage yourself and other people's customers, knowledge, ability, efforts, money and resources.

To achieve this comes the need to determine your special talents, skills, competencies, abilities and strengths and focus on developing them to a higher level on you and your business well. How do you pick a name? You have three options. The first is to pick a name that says exactly what your business is. Begin with what your business is going to do and the image you want to express.

Include both in the actual name of the business or reflect those ideas in the name, so that when people hear your business name, they know what you are offering. Be sure the name is not already in local use and that it is not too similar to that of a competitor. Try to pick one that is catchy and memorable; alliteration often works well. Also, be sure to pick a name that is not difficult to pronounce or spell. When people call directory assistance, you want them to be able to find you.

After you come up with five names that you really like, get some feedback from people you trust; they may not think your name is as good as you think it is. Remember, your business has to serve a market need, so finding out what the market thinks about your proposed business name, even in a small and informal way, is smart. The second method of business-name creation is to pick a name that is totally unique and has nothing to do with your business at all. Choose names that are great because they are so unique that they are memorable.

The risk here is that while your name may be unique, it may be too odd and obscure for people to remember it. Trademark Concerns While making your final decision regarding your name, it is important to do a trademark search to see if the name already has been trademarked. If it has, you may not be able to use it.

Different names are given different degrees of trademark protection. A trademark is a distinctive word, phrase, or logo that is used to identify a business. Nike and its unique swoosh symbol are protected under trademark law because they are moved by multitudes or by popular opinion.

If all the prophets in the world prophesy you into a successful great business and God has not ordained that business will fail. I have not sent these prophets yet they ran. I Have not spoken to them yet they prophesied (Jeremiah 23:21)

Many people are running a race they have not been assigned to run and results are failure. If you go into businesses that God has not confirmed or ordained be assured that you will finance that business yourself. So stop being led by men, rather, be led by God. If you let God lead you, then you shall not want!

No amount of confirmation by people can put words into His mouth. What He has not said, He has not said; what He has not written, He has not written. Locate His writing about you, not writings of men. Human confirmation is, more often than not, confusion is disguise.

Choosing Great Names and Locations

Now that you have a good idea about what your business is going to be and where you are headed with it, it is time to begin to put your foundation in place. You will need to structure the business legally, get the necessary licenses and permits, and get funding.

But before you can do any of those things, it is time to have some fun. You need to name your business and, in all likelihood, find a location for it. Remember Location, Location, and Location. What's in a Name? Naming your business should be enjoyable, but for some people, it is stressful. What if you pick the wrong name? What if the name you pick has already been taken? While it is smart to be cautious, it is nothing to get overly concerned about.

The important thing to realize is that your business name will become your alter ego, so be sure to pick a name that reflects personal assets. Your home, cars, bank accounts, everything is at risk when you are a sole proprietor. Another problem with this form of business is that you have no partners to work with or bounce ideas off of.

It is a dangerous way to do business. Therefore, having a teammate is why operating a business as a partnership is attractive. Essentially, a business partnership is a lot like a marriage. You need to pick a good partner because you will be spending a lot of time together and trusting each other. And, as with a sole proprietorship, in a general partnership, both you and your partner are personally liable for the debts of the business.

The danger is that your partner can make some dumb decisions and get the partnership into debt, and you will be personally responsible for that debt. So, as you can see, while there are many good aspects to having a partner, partnerships are fraught with danger.

You have to weigh the benefits against the burdens and decide if bringing in a partner is right for you. Another thing to be wary of is the emotional aspect of having a partner. One advantage to being a sole proprietor, and thus the only boss, is you have no one to answer to except yourself. That's one of the definite perks of being a solo entrepreneur. Bringing in a partner means you will have to consider another point of view before any major decision is made.

Also, when partnerships do not work out, best friends who become partners do not always stay best friends. On the other side of the ledger, there are many things to be said for having a business partner. One is that it enables you to have someone with whom to brainstorm. That great idea you have may not be such a great idea after all, and a partner you trust can tell you why.

A partner also gives you another pair of hands to do the work. It is difficult to be the one who has to do everything when you are solo. Partners alleviate that. Last, and certainly not least, having a business distinctive. Other words are given far less protection.

Common or ordinary words that are not inherently distinctive get much less, or no, trademark protection, even if someone tries to trademark them. Licenses, Permits, and Business Formation Deciding what legal form your business should take is not the most scintillating of topics, but it may be one of the most important decisions you will make.

The form your business takes can determine how big it may grow, who can invest in it, and who is responsible should it get in trouble. It is a critical decision. Once decided, it is then important to handle some other legal issues, namely getting the requisite licenses and permits required by your city, county, or state.

Business Formation

There are three forms your business can take. It can be a sole proprietorship, a partnership, or a corporation, and each of the last two have subsets. When deciding which of these is best for you, it would behoove you to speak with both your lawyer and your account, because each choice has different legal and financial considerations to weigh.

Below is an overview that you can use as a launching pad for discussions with your own advisors.

- **Sole Proprietorships and General Partnerships**

A sole proprietorship is the cheapest and easiest form of business you can start. Simply decide on a name for your business, get a business license, file and publish a fictitious business name statement, hang your shingle, and voilà! You are in business.

The downside to sole proprietorship is significant: You and the business are legally the same thing. If something goes wrong, say as a chiropractor you accidentally injure someone, not only is your business at risk, but so you run the show and make the decisions.

A limited partner cannot incur obligations on behalf of the partnership and does not participate in the daily operations and management of the partnership. In fact, the participation of a limited partner in the partnership is usually nothing more than initially contributing capital and hopefully later receiving a proportionate share of the profits.

A limited partner is essentially a passive investor. While the general partner has all of the power, he or she also has the lion's share of the liability. A limited partner's liability is capped at the amount of his or her financial contribution to the partnership. Should the truck of a limited partnership kill someone accidentally, the damaged party could go after the general partner's personal, but would be limited to the limited partner's capital contribution.

Thus, the main advantage to this business entity is that it allows the general partner the freedom to run the business without interference, and gives the limited partners diminished liability if things go wrong.

Although a limited partner may seek to be more involved in the day-to-day operations of the partnership, he or she does so at some risk.

If he or she does participate more, it is altogether possible that he or she may be viewed as a general partner in the eyes of the law, with its attendant liability risks. Another key benefit of the limited partnership is that it pays no income tax. Income and losses are attributed proportionally to each partner and accounted for on their respective tax returns.

Because of this flow-through tax treatment, a limited partnership is often the structure of choice for real estate ventures and investment securities groups. If you do decide to start your business as a limited partnership, have your partnership agreement drafted by an attorney.

Partner gives you someone to share the financial responsibilities of the business. That is not insignificant. Having considered the pros and cons, having concluded that a partner can help more than it might hurt, and maybe even knowing someone you would like to partner with, it is still a good idea that you "date" first before jumping in. Find a project or two and work together. See how you get along, how your styles mesh (or don't), how you deal with deadlines, and whether the union enhances your work.

Remember, you will be spending a lot of time with your partner, so you need to be sure that you work well together, have a good time, and have skills that complement one another. Finally, get some work references and make some phone calls. Deciding to partner with someone is one of the most important decisions you can make in your small business, so don't skimp on the homework.

As far as the costs go, the licensing and permits are fairly insignificant. The main cost is hiring a business lawyer to draft the partnership agreement. • Limited Partnerships There are two classes of partnerships: general partnerships (discussed above) and limited partnerships. In a general partnership, all partners are equal.

Each partner has equal power to incur obligations on behalf of the partnership, and each partner has unlimited liability for the debts of that partnership. Because not all partnerships require that the partners have equal power and liabilities, some partnerships decide to form as a limited partnership instead. In a limited partnership, there is usually only one general partner (although there could be more).

The other partners are called limited partners, hence the name limited partnership. In a limited partnership, the general partner or partners have full management responsibility and control of the partnership business on a day-to-day basis.

As the general partner you to be more effective and, thus, more productive from the get-go. Computers represent a solid investment of your startup capital. Don't skimp in this area. Throughout this book you have been, and will be, cautioned to keep your overhead low. High overhead will eat up your profits and your precious cash flow quickly. But this is not one of those times.

The rapid pace of technological change means that computers usually become obsolete within three or four years. If you buy a used one, or an older or a slower model, you are simply speeding up the moment when you will have to buy a new one. Be smart and buy a good computer and the necessary software now.

You have likely learned a thing or two about purchasing computers since you bought your first one. You are more knowledgeable about your computer needs, and you probably know what areas you would like to improve. It may be that your monitor is too small and you want a larger one, or that you want a newer operating system. Probably what you want is speed and more speed.

Creating a Great Image

At the height of the e-commerce boom, an executive from a well established "old-economy" company was hired to be the new CEO of a young, brash, well-financed Internet startup. For his first day at his new company, the CEO decided to look his best. He dressed in an expensive suit and his favorite tie. That day, he was to address the company's 100-plus employees. As he tells the story, he felt sharp, and looked great.

The new CEO gave an enthusiastic, short introductory speech and then opened the floor to questions. The room was utterly and completely silent. Seconds seemed like hours as people refused to participate. "Come on," he implored, "ask me a question." Finally, someone yelled out, "Why are you wearing a tie?"

- **Incorporating (Starting your own company)**

The best thing about forming your business as a corporation is that it limits your personal liability, which is not true for partnerships and sole proprietorships. For example, say that you owned a tire shop and one of your employees negligently installed a tire that fell off a car and caused a three-car accident with several personal injuries. If your tire store was not a corporation, the injured parties could come after you personally for monetary damages.

This means that you could lose your business, your house—everything. That would not be true if you incorporated. Creditors are limited to the assets of the corporation only for payment and may not collect directly from the shareholders.

There are several types of corporations including limited liability companies, closely held corporations, professional corporations, S and C corporations.

Outfitting the Office The actual process of setting up your business will involve dealing with plenty of details—details that must be understood and organized before you open the doors; details that must be handled and forgotten so that you can go onto other, more important matters; details that can sink or swim your business.

Automating Your Office

Whatever your business, you must computerize it. Whether it involves tracking sales, writing letters, or inventory control, starting out with a good computer system is vital. Although it may seem less expensive to do certain office tasks by hand rather than investing in a good computer system or related software, that is fuzzy logic for two reasons.

First, you eventually will automate whatever tasks you begin by hand. Changing over later will take longer and cost more. Second, computer hardware and software will allow to hire someone to do it for you. If you decide to design your own logo, you will need a software program that offers graphics, clip art, and photographs that can be incorporated into your logo. It is important that you not use any material that is copyrighted in your logo design. If you can afford to hire someone to create a logo for you, do it.

Elements of Your Image

These items need to be coordinated and thematic in order to create a dynamic business identity and image: Your Brochure. Not every business will need or use a brochure. Even if a brochure is not traditionally part of businesses like yours, it still might be a great way to create a professional image and bring in business.

The thing to be wary of is spending money on a brochure if it really does nothing to add to your business. A brochure can be an expensive item and thus not worth the money if you really don't need it. When creating a brochure, avoid the following: Making it too busy.

Creating a brochure that is so jam packed with information that it is unpleasing to the eye and difficult to read is a sure way to waste money. It is much better to keep paragraphs short, use white space, use bullets, and keep it simple.

Making the cover boring

Too many businesses think that headlining their brochure with their business name is a sure way to entice people to read more. If you want people to read your brochure, you must catch their attention (usually with some benefit they could get by reading more) and draw them in. Ask yourself: What is the purpose of this brochure? Is it an introduction to your business, a selling tool, both, or more?

Whatever your answer your brochure needs to reflect ness too. After someone encounters you and your business for the first time, they will leave with an impression. It may be positive, it may be negative. They may think yours is a well-run, professional enterprise that will provide them with a great service, or not.

One thing you can bank on though is that the first impression will very likely be the lens that they use to view your company forever. Think about it in your own life. If you meet someone for the first time and he acts like a real jerk, don't you label him a jerk? It doesn't matter that he might have been having a bad day.

He becomes "the jerk." When you go to a business for the first time and get bad service, don't you usually conclude that their business doesn't deserve your continued patronage? That is why they say that you only have one chance to make a great first impression. The Importance of a Great Image Although image isn't everything, it is not insignificant. Your signs, business cards, letterhead, logo, and store/office say much about who you are. Combined, these things constitute your business identity.

A professional business identity says that, even though you are new, you are to be taken seriously. Of course, you will have to back up that great image with great products or services and customer service. But to get people to understand that yours is a business worth patronizing, you have to open the door by having a sharper image.

That is the task before you. Your Logo A logo is one of the first things you need to create because it will be used on your letterhead, business cards, and other documents. It will distinguish your company, set a tone, and foster your desired image. You want a logo that exemplifies who you are and what it is you do.

When creating a logo, you have two options: you can do it yourself or load. Inside, your business addresses and contact information should be easy to find. Features and benefits of working with you should be prominent. Beyond that, what you do with your site is up to you. You may want to consider having some features that keep people coming back, because the more they come back to your site, the more likely it is they will buy from you. You can offer such things as: interactivity.

E-commerce interactivity means providing interactive tools that enable potential customers to learn more about your products. It could also mean offering chat rooms, message boards, or newsletters. Streaming video is a possibility.

Members Only Areas

Some businesses offer members only domains on their Web sites, where they offer access to premium information, tools, and services. Think about

AOL for a moment. It is nothing but a huge members only Web site; not a bad model.

Content

On the Internet, content is king. A site without good, arresting, useful, timely content is a site that is probably going nowhere. Think about the sites you like. What is it that draws you there? In all likelihood, good content is near the top of your list. Where do you get your content? You can write it yourself or hire someone to create content for you. the same values, tone, and theme that will be found in your other image-creating materials. Use your logo. Use your colors. Reinforce your desired image with text and graphics that reflect your business image.

Signs

A big, bold, visible sign in the right location(s) can be one of the best tools for creating an image, as well as generating new business. Signs are obviously most used for retail businesses, especially when drop-in traffic is a key element to your business model. Signs come in many forms, from cheap wood ones to expensive electrical and glass models. T

The same considerations that are used in your other materials apply here. If you can get the image of each of your materials to reinforce an overall theme, busy people who don't yet know of your business will easily understand what it is you are about if they are met with consistency. Choosing the right sign especially is an area where professional expertise is useful. How big should the sign be?

What should it say? How big should the letters be? Creative and Design companies will help you figure this all out.

Your Web Site

Even if your business has nothing to do with the Internet, you cannot pass up the chance to create an online image. Indeed, a Web site has become a business necessity. Not only is it an inexpensive way to buttress your image and tell people who you are, but it is also an opportunity to sell more, get more customers, make more money, and impress strangers. And you need not be Amazon.com to be successful.

In fact, you probably don't want to be. Your business Website should, in all likelihood, be a clean, simple, elegant place that does a few things very well. Your home page should explain what your business is and what the Web site is about. It should be simple and easy to manage.

CHAPTER 6

It's Not About Money. Start with What You Have

This is a chapter that encourages anyone who has a burning desire to start a business but he or she has insufficient startup capital. My advice to you is, do not worry start with what you have. Three things are important at this level. First, you must have a clear strategic vision answering three strategic questions: where am I? Where do I want to be? And how do I get there? Second, is to craft a mission statement clearly explaining the business scope which must answer the following questions: who we are? What we do? And why are we in business? Third is the financial education from which you will be able to use financial intelligence.

On one hand while strategic vision is the description of the road map or the unfolding of your tomorrow, it is simply an idea. On the other hand, it is the financial intelligence that solves money problems which includes the lack of adequate capital to start your own business.

You can emulate my example.

When I decided to be a writer, I just started writing. Then I finally realized the obvious: if you want to be a writer, start writing! Writing is free, and no one needs to bestow a title of writer upon you to begin writing. The same is true with art, business, travel, and plenty of other fields.

If you want to start a business, all you need is one idea. The idea does not need to be big; sometimes small ideas make great small businesses. Think about one thing you know how to do that other people would also like to know about. This means that, *to identify what type of business you will be able to do, is simple and easy. Just do research and find out the problem that is in your area and think about the solution to that problem. It is that solution that will turn to be your greatest idea from which you can base your decision to start your own business.*

Use What You Have

One day I was reading a book and the writer said,"My biggest challenge is in keeping focused on myself and avoiding the unhelpful comparison with others. I know it is essential to do this and yet it is incredibly hard to practice". Based on what this writer said I can conclude that the death of contentment is comparison.

Comparisons are generally unhelpful since:

1) We are only likely to compare ourselves to others whose achievements dwarf our own and hence make ourselves feel bad in the process. It would be fine if we sought their example as inspiration to work hard to get there, but most people (myself included) use the comparison as a means of beating ourselves up for not being where we would like to be.
2) We only see the publically shared information that represents the highs, the good-points and the accomplishments. Nobody really shares the downs, the failures or the difficulties, only the bits they are proud of which will inflate their ego. If only we could remember this when comparing ourselves to them, we might feel better about how we measure up.
3) We donot recognize all the years of hard work, disappointments, the failures and the occasional good-fortune that resulted in their achievements.

Using what we have means maintaining an inward focus on making the best use of our own time, skills, potential and attention rather than being driven by factors outside of our influence. Progress towards our goals each day, depends on how we apply our skills, time and resources, the actions we take, the decisions we make and the distractions we resist. It all comes down to us.

Do What You Can

Resisting distraction and comparison, focusing attention upon taking action and accepting our starting point as the launching pad for the process of creation are all essential if we are to free ourselves to take action and get on with the process of doing business.

Sure, we may wish for more favorable conditions. Our starting point may be non-ideal. Progress so far may well have been rocky, or non-existent to this point. Regardless of all these factors, we have the choice to accept them and to act regardless, or to use them as further sources of despondency and justifications for inaction. It is a battle I fight with myself daily, but I know that it feels better when I choose the path of action. I hope the same is true to you. A common question many of us ask is this: How do I get from where I am to where I want to be if there is nothing to build on in the first place?

For example, you want to start a business, but you have no experience in business development. You want to shift to a different career field, but you donot have knowledge in the area. You want to be at the top in what you do but you have no know-how in the area. You want to let go of your past and start on a new journey, but there is nothing for you to start off with. And if you cannot create something, you cannot get anything.

If you have ever felt this way about your goals, there are a few points I want to share with you.

There Are Many Successful People Who Start From Nothing

The first thing I want to point out is that many people start from nothing. While there are rich people who start from a position of power and wealth, there are many successful people from poor families, just as there are people who lead lackadaisical lives despite having a lot of wealth. Instead of talking about money here, I want to focus the discussion on one's personal achievements and knowledge, because these are arguably what shape one's life success.

The second point I want to make is to invite you to rethink the notion that you have nothing. Because every time you think you have nothing, it is likely the opposite. It is the proverbial notion of whether the glass is half-empty or half-full. There is always something there. The pessimist sees the glass as half-empty; the optimist sees the glass as half-full.

Have you ever considered that the glass has always been all full though? The bottom half is filled with water and the top half is filled with air. If you donot see what you have today as something, it is possible that you have been living in your own reality for too long, to the point where you take what you have for granted. You have developed a mental blindness to the value of what you have. It is a matter of re-tuning yourself to recognize those things you do have.

Try mentally swapping positions with someone who is in a worse-off situation than you. It can be someone who just got robbed, someone who just got retrenched, a convict sentenced for life behind bars, a patient suffering from a terminal illness with a month to live, a vegetable, a person with anterograde amnesia, a starving beggar with no home to go to, a bankrupt, someone with heavy debt to clear, a famine-stricken child in Africa, etc. — the possibilities are endless. How would you feel? What would you become? What would life be like compared to what you have now?

Suddenly, it is apparent that there are so many things in your life you didnot realize. All the things you have from before that you saw as nothing suddenly becomes something. Things like your senses, your health, your freedom, your livelihood, your rights, your friends, your family, your knowledge, your skill sets, your abilities, your intellect, and many more elements begin to make sense.

All these are real things, real tools that you possess. They are assets beyond any doubt. There are many people who wish they had these, yet they donot. Realize it or not, by being able to see this post, you are in a better place than many people in this world. *And focusing on the things that you do have now and making the best out of them are surer ways to move you forward in life than not recognizing them.*

Your Problems Are Something Too

In fact, everything you have in your life now is something. Including your problems, contrary to what many would think. I know many of you may be thinking, *'how can my problems be of value? They weigh me down. I wish I could get rid of all my life problems immediately.'*

There was something I read in **Think and Grow Rich** years ago that I want to share with you. Many people always see their problems as liabilities, and the things they have as assets. However, have you ever realized that your problems are actually your assets too — in fact, bigger assets than you realize? Because for every problem you face, hundreds of thousands of people around the world are probably facing it too. And if your problem is so huge that it's weighing on you, imagine how many people would want to know the solution to this problem. Who is a better person to discover the solution than you, the person who is in the middle of it all?

Once you find the solution, imagine how valuable this solution will be to others who have the same problem. It is a huge asset! *Your problems are really your assets in disguise. They are your hidden gold mines waiting to be mined and converted into gold.* In fact, our problems are the keys to abundance. It is with these problems that you become a richer person, not just in terms of physical wealth, but also emotionally, mentally and spiritually.

And Then There Is Something Else

And even beyond your problems/liabilities, assets, knowledge, abilities, and skill sets, there is something else that you have. Even if you have nothing to your name, even if you have been declared bankrupt, even if you are million dollars in debt, even if everyone has left you in this world, even if you are to lose your job/status/knowledge/achievements, even if your life has been decimated, you still have something.

CHAPTER 7

Design and Market Your Great Brands

Marketing is both a philosophy of business and an important function in the operation of a company. Marketing is concerned with making profits by providing customers satisfaction. ***Thus, when people buy products or services they do not want the products or service per se, they want the benefits from using the products or services.*** Products and services help to solve customers' problems. It is the solutions to these problems that customers are really buying.

Development of Present-Day Marketing

In early industrial and commercial developments, the emphasis was placed on production. Demand was high and all that was manufactured could be sold without difficulty. Later the emphasis switched to sales. With reduction in consumer demand, effort had to be made to sell factory output

Roughly the period from the 1920s to the 1950s, was characterized by this sales orientation. Thus, sales and advertising were the activities receiving most emphasis. Latter from the 1950s to the present day with ever increasing competitor activity and consumer needs and wants should initiate the production process.

Thus, a marketing orientation developed and this is the current situation. However, it is important to recognize that not all organizations adapted the marketing orientation and, in most cases, corporate failure can be directly attributed to companies having a production orientation approach.

Characteristics of Organizations Having Production Orientation

- ✓ Demand is a function of supply
- ✓ There is an emphasis on production
- ✓ The firm has an inward-looking approach
- ✓ Most things made can be sold
- ✓ Buyers are sensitive to price
- ✓ Market must have low cost
- ➢ With sales orientation, selling the output of production becomes the most important activity

Characteristics of Organization Having Marketing Orientation

- • Scarcity of markets
- • A focus on customers
- • An outward looking approach
- • High level of competitor activity
- • Supply exceeds demand

Organizations adopting a marketing orientation or the marketing concept are therefore interested in the satisfaction of consumer needs and wants at a profit.

The Market Concept

Marketing concept is concerned with satisfying consumer needs and wants at a profit. Therefore, business is about satisfying customers at a profit. So, any company implementing the marketing concept will achieve their corporate objectives by identifying and satisfying the needs and want of a target markets more effectively than competitors. Effective marketing starts with the recognition of customer needs and then works backwards to devise products or services to satisfy these needs.

In this way marketing managers can satisfy customers more efficiently in the present and anticipate changes in customer needs more accurately in the future. This means that organizations should focus on building long term customer relations in which the initial sale is viewed as a beginning step in the process, not as an end goal.

What Marketing is all about?

Marketing is defined as the process of planning and executing conception, pricing, promotion and distribution of ideas, goods and services to create exchanges that satisfy individual and organizational goals.

Marketing is the performance of activities that seek to accomplish an organization's objectives by anticipating customer or client needs and directing a flow of need satisfying goods and services from producer to customer or client. Marketing is the management process responsible for identifying, anticipating and satisfying consumers' requirements profitably. Therefore, marketing is more than selling and advertising.

The Marketing Mix

Marketing involves making a number of interrelated decisions about various aspects of company activity, which have a major impact on success or failure of the company as a business enterprise. The term marketing mix is used to denote the range of activities within the framework of marketing decision making.

The marketing mix is the set of controllable variables that must be managed to satisfy the target market and achieve organizational objectives. For convenience, the market mix is divided into four major decision areas: Product Decisions, Price Decisions, Promotion Decisions and Place Decisions

Product Decisions

- These include the number, type, brand grouping and quality of company products, their sizes, variety and form of packing.
- Decisions on whether to add new products, phase out products, restyle or rebrand fall into this category.

2. Price Decisions

- These include the discount structure, the relationship of price between product sizes, the general pricing policy and the pricing of new products.

3. Promotion Decisions

- These include advertising strategy, media selection, copy writing, public relations, personal selling and special sales promotions, all involving the conveyance of information about the company

4. Place Decisions

- These include decisions relating to the distribution channels and the appointment of agents among other things

The effective use of the marketing tools within the marketing mix is an interrelated manner and is the key to successful marketing and profitable business.

Marketing Management

We have identified the main elements of the marketing mix as: Product; Price; Promotion and Place. The aim of marketing management is to get the right product of the right quality to right place at the right price using the right promotional methods. Marketing management is therefore the process of putting into practice the marketing mix-known as the 4Ps.

To manage this process it involves analysis, planning and control:

1. Analysis

As we have seen, a marketing orientation begins and ends with the customer. Thus, analysis in marketing management involves finding the answers to the following questions:

- ✓ Who are our customers and potential customers?
- ✓ Who do they buy (or not buy)
- ✓ Do they buy our product or service?
- ✓ When do they buy it?
- ✓ Where do they buy it?
- ✓ How do they buy it?
- ✓ Having bought the product are they satisfied with it?
- ✓ How are customer needs changing?
- ✓ Which of the competitor's products do they consider buying?

2. Planning

Marketing management also involves using the information gained from market analysis to plan the organization's marketing response/activities.

3. Control

The third main component of marketing management is to control the operationalization of the marketing plan. Control involves setting measurable targets for the plan and then checking performance against these targets. If necessary, remedial action will need to be taken to ensure that planned and actual performances are brought into line.

Internal Marketing

As part of the overall marketing process of delivering customer satisfaction it is important that the whole corporate effort is coordinated and committed to achieving this objective. In practice, this means that all employees at all levels should appreciate not only the reason for the firm's existence; but also that each and every employee has a responsibility to understand the concept of customer or marketing orientation and the importance of their individual contribution.

CHAPTER 8

Understanding Staffing Issues

The practice of human resource management (HRM) is concerned with all aspects of how people are employed and managed in organizations. It covers activities such as strategic HRM, human capital management, corporate social responsibility, knowledge management, organization management, resourcing (human resource planning, recruitment and selection and talent management), performance management, learning and development, reward management, Employee relations, Health and safety and Provision of employee services.

Stone (2010) defines Human Resource Management as a productive use of people to achieve strategic business objectives and satisfy individual employee needs. According to Armstrong (2009) Human Resource Management is a strategic, integrated and coherent approach to the employment, development and well being of the people working in organizations.

The Matching Model

One of the first explicit statements of the HRM concepts was made by the Michigan School (Tichy and Devanna, 1984) They held that HR systems and the organization structure should be managed in a way that is congruent with organizational strategy (hence the name "matching model"

They further explained that there is a human resource cycle (an adaptation of which is illustrated in Figure 8.1 below.

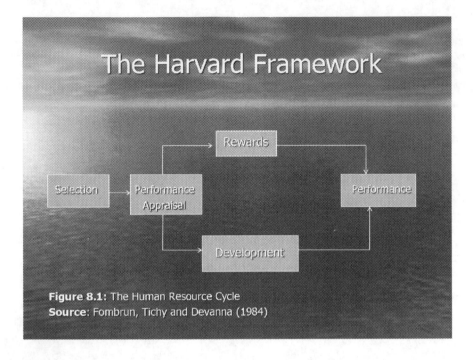

Figure 8.1: The Human Resource Cycle
Source: Fombrun, Tichy and Devanna (1984)

It consists of four generic processes or functions that are performed in all organizations. These are:

- ➤ selection – matching available huma resources to jobs
- ➤ appraisal – performance management
- ➤ rewards – the reward system is one of the most under – utilized and mishandled managerial tools for driving organizational performance;
- ➤ It must reward short as well as long - term achievements, bearing in mind that business must perform in the present to succeed in the future
- ➤ development – developing high quality employees

Your success in business will be determined by the people who will work for you more than any other factor. At the same time every business is subject to labour market forces over which it has little or no control.

There is likely to be a "buyer's market" for some job categories and a "seller's market" for others. Thus, a company must do its best to identify which employees-or employee agents represent the highest value to the organization and then apply its resources in a manner that optimizes their retention in a free labour market place.

On one hand one of the realities of market – wise retention is that you will never be able to keep all employees – particularly the most talented, who have the greatest mobility. People retire. They are "poached" by rival companies. More than a few entrepreneurial types go into business for themselves.

Others simply find opportunities that your business can not much. Some businesses create employee turnover as a matter of policy. In the end the struggle to retain good employees is a losing game. Either by death, retirement, defection, everyone eventually leaves.

The most you can hope for is to have some influence over who leaves and when. On the other hand comes hiring of former employees. Thomas Wolfe's message that you can't go home again does not hold true for former employees. Just because a valued person has left your company, don't assume that he or she is gone for good. Some women drop out while their children are infants but are ready to return a few years later.

Others leave for what appear to be great career moves, only to be disappointed and disillusioned. Rehires can a valuable asset for your company. First, they know your business and how to get things done there. This gives them a huge advantage over people hired from the outside, who generally need many months to learn the ropes and become effective.

Second rehires return with broader experience and, in many cases, new skills. Finally, every returning defector sends a loud and clear message to others that the grass isn't greener elsewhere. Worth to note that the best businesses have the best people. Success requires excellent performance of each team member. Great people are excellent at their work, they accept high levels of responsibility, they have a positive mental attitude, they use their time very well and get along with others.

Your ability to find and hire the right and great people is the key to leveraging and multiplying yourself. At this level think through results expected, skills required, personality attributes necessary, write out the job description, cast a wide net, look for achievement history, sense of urgency, intelligent questions, check resumes and references personally, hire slow, fire fast and start them off right and strong. The concept of hiring and retention are two sides of the same coin.

They complement each other, and if both are done well they produce what every business desperately needs: first-class human assets. Retention is the converse of turnover – the turnover being the sum of voluntary and involuntary separations between an employee and his or her business. Retention isn't simply a "feel good" issue.

Retention

The retention of good employees matters for three important bottom – line reasons:

- The growing importance of intellectual capital;
- A causal link between employee turnover; and
- The high cost of employee turnover. What makes retention so challenging is that it is complicated by a number of factors: demographics conditions; cultural expectations and upheavals in the world of work.

Retention is especially challenging when the work force is highly diverse. And this is the type of work force that managers in many parts of the world today face. Businesses can best improve their retention rates by crafting creative, specialized strategies for each major segment of the work force. Every great business has a distribution of low, average, and high performers. Nevertheless most corporate retention programs –which are typically expensive to implement.

CHAPTER 9

Understanding Numbers

You need to walk before you run. Understanding numbers or figures is ultimate if you are to make an impact in business. It is important to know the difference between assets and liabilities. It is very surprising that in many cases the poor buy liabilities but they think they are assets. You need to know good expenses and bad expenses and also good liabilities and bad liabilities.

Financial Reporting

In financial reporting we normally deal with financial statements that an organization's accounting system produces including the profit and loss account also commonly called Income Statement, the balance sheet and cash flow statements.

The income statement presents the financial performance the balance sheet presents the financial position while cash flow represents the financial adaptability. Out of the three financial statements the balance sheet which represents assets, capital and liabilities shows how the business is financed.

Show Me the Money

Finding the funds to start your business is usually one of the most challenging things the budding entrepreneur will face. Whether yours is a small, home-based business or a large venture that requires six- or seven-figure funding, the good news is that money is available.

The bad news is that it is sometimes harder to secure than you may anticipate such as legal and accounting costs. You may need to hire a lawyer to help you negotiate contracts, incorporate, or perform other legal services. An accountant may be needed to set up your books.

Working capital is the money you will need to keep your business going until you start to make a profit. The old adage "it takes money to make money" is true and real. It is critical to have enough working capital on hand to cover the following costs: Debt payments. If you will be borrowing money to get started, you will want to begin repaying it right away.

Service businesses have little, if any inventory, but retail and wholesale companies often spend large sums in this area. Business finance therefore deals with deciding the capital structure. Capital structure explains how the business is financed. Businesses are either financed either by equity capital or debt capital.

These are the main sources of finance. However, each of these has cost of acquisitioning the funds. Thus if funds are acquired from equity holders the business will pay cost of equity to its shareholders and if funds have been acquired from lenders of finance such as banks the business pays cost of debt normally this is an interest. Although debt is a way of financing a business in many cases the financial institutions such as banks do not provide the funds to a newly established business because normally banks look for financial statement or collateral of which the business might not have because it is just starting.

So this leaves only one option of financing the business that is just starting with equity funds. Since they are two options for financing the business: equity or debt you can also decide to obtain the funds from both equity holders (your own funds) and the banks at the same time.

Therefore in most cases, a company's funds may be viewed as a pool of resource. But look around. Every one of those businesses that you see as you drive down the street began as someone's dream and, somehow, those entrepreneurs found the money to open their doors. If they did, so can you. New businesses normally have difficult time securing money for a variety of reasons.

Conventional financing may be difficult because a new business is a risk to banks— there is no track record or assets to go on. For this reason, almost 75 percent of all start-up businesses are funded through other means. In this chapter, those other options are examined.

Money and the New Business

The very first thing required of you is to accurately estimate the amount of money you need. Taking a cold, hard look at your money requirements will help you know your business better and help ensure your success. Once you know how much capital your business will require, it will be incumbent on you to get it.

Having a cash crunch from the start is a sure way to go out of business fast. Moreover, a realistic budget will help convince a lender or investor that you understand your business and are worth the risk. The first thing any investor will want to know is how much money you will need and how you plan to spend it. They will want specific details on how the money will be spent and how you plan to repay the money.

How much money do you need?

If you have created a business plan, you should have a pretty good idea how much money you will need to get started. If you haven't figured it out yet, this section will help you. The money you will need can be divided into three categories: one-time costs, working capital, and ongoing costs. One-time costs are things that you will need to spend money on to star your business but will unlikely see again.

Chapter 10

Understanding Business Law

Business Law: Law of Contract

What Contract is all about?

A contract is an agreement between two or more parties that creates obligation on them that law will recognize and enforce. **All contracts are agreements but not all agreements are contracts.** The enforceability of the agreement arises from the moral premise that an individual who voluntarily assumes an obligation that creates expectations in others should fulfill that obligation.

If he does not do so, the other party should be allowed to recover compensation for any loss or damage that he may suffer because of the non – fulfillment of the obligation so assumed. Thus, for there to be a valid contract, there must be at least the following five (5) essentials:

Essentials of a Valid Contract

Agreement

An agreement which is enforceable as a contract may be oral or in writing. This is because there are generally no legal requirements that an agreement should be in writing for it to be treated by law as a legally binding contract. As a result, an agreement will be enforced by law as a contract even though it is not in writing at all. In fact, the largest number of contracts are never in writing. They are oral. The method which the courts determine whether an agreement has been reached is to enquire whether one party has made an offer which the other party has accepted. As stated earlier for most types of contract, the offer and acceptance may be made orally in writing or they may be implied from the conduct of the parties.

Offer

An offer can be described as an expression of willingness by one person (the Offeror) to enter into a contract with another person (the Offeree) made with an intention that it should be binding on the Offeror as soon as it is accepted by the Offeree. Thus, if for example, A person goes into a shop, picks up a bottle of coke and walks to the paying counter with money in his hands. That is an offer to buy the drink. Consequently, if the shop attendant accepts the money in payment for the coke, a contract will have been concluded between him and the shop for the sale of the Coke.

Invitation to Offers

However, it should be noted that not every apparent offer will be regarded as such by law. Some words or conduct which may appear to be offers are not offers at all. For example, an advertisement of goods for sale is not an offer of the goods for sale. Similarly, the display of goods in a shop window or on a shop shelf is also not an offer of the goods for sale.

Termination of an Offer

An offer will not constitute an agreement unless it is accepted before it is terminated by the Offeror. As a result, where the Offeree purports to accept an offer that has already been terminated, his/her acceptance will not be valid to convert the offer into an agreement between him and the Offeror. An offer can be terminated through the following ways:

(a) Counter Offer
(b) Revocation
(c) Rejection
(d) Lapse of Time
(e) Un occurrence of an event

Acceptance

An offer cannot constitute an agreement unless it is first accepted by the Offeree. In other words, it is the combination of an offer and acceptance that creates an agreement which will be enforced as a contract. *Under the law of contract, an acceptance is defined as a final and unqualified expression of assent to the terms of an offer.*

Communication of Acceptance

Generally, an acceptance must be communicated to the Offeror so that in the absence of that, there will be no contract. In other words, the acceptance must be brought to the Offeror's notice. Accordingly, there is no contract where the Offeree writes his acceptance of the offer on a piece of paper which he keeps himself.

Consideration

Although there may be a valid agreement constituted by an offer which is accepted, the agreement may not be enforced as a contract in the absence of 'consideration'. Consideration shall mean something of value in the eyes of law. The basis of this rule is the fact that courts are not willing to enforce gratuitous promises as contracts.

For this purpose, consideration is either some benefit to the Offeror or some detriment to the Offeree. Thus, payment by the buyer is consideration for the seller's delivery. Conversely, delivery or promise of delivery by the seller is consideration for the buyer's payment or promise of payment. This can be described either as a detriment to the seller or as a benefit to the buyer

In law of contract past, consideration is no consideration at all. For this reason, payment for past services is generally not contractually binding as valid consideration unless the services were rendered on the premise that the payment would be made at some future date

Privity of Contract

Because of the importance of consideration in the enforcement of a contract, generally only parties to a contract will be allowed to enforce it. In other words, a person who is not a party to contract (i.e. who has not provided consideration) will not be allowed to enforce the contract even if it was concluded for his benefit. For example, if a father enters into a contract to buy a car for his son and the seller refuses to deliver the vehicle after payment, the son cannot sue the seller for the delivery of the car. Only the father who has given consideration for the sale has that right.

Terms of Contract

When one party to a contract brings a court action against the other party, it is often on the ground that the latter has failed to fulfill his obligation under the contract. Now whether a party to a contract is under any contractual obligation depends on whether performance of that obligation is part of, or a term of, the contract.

1. Express

A term of contract is express if it is orally agreed upon by the parties at the time of concluding the contract or is contained in a written document embodying the contract.

2. Implied

A term may also be implied. It will be implied by conduct where even though they may not specifically have discussed it or agreed on it. They should, as reasonable people be taken to have intended that it should be part of the contract. For example, in a contract of employment, whether the parties specifically agreed on it or not, it will be implied that the employee should be paid his salary in full in any month if he is absent from work without permission or reasonable cause. Similarly, if it is customary in any industry that employees should receive a bonus at a certain point in time, that will be a term implied into their contracts of employment

Lastly, law implies a number of terms into specific contracts. For instance, it is an implied term in a contract for the sale of goods that the goods should fit for their intended use. Again, it is an implied term of a contract of employment that the employee should be entitled to a certain number of days every year as his annual leave

Conditions and Warranties

A term of contract (whether express or implied) may be a condition of the contract or a mere warranty, whether it is one or the other may depend on how it is called by the parties in their agreement. Generally, a condition is such an important term of contract that its breach by one party deprives the other of a substantial benefit of the contract so that he is entitled, if he so wishes, to regard himself as discharged from further performance of the contract. A warranty is a minor term so that its breach does not entitle the innocent party to consider himself discharged from further performance of the contract.

Discharge of a Contract

A party to a contract may be discharged (i.e., released) from further performance of the contract by the following factors.

1. **Mutual Agreement**
   This will happen where, after their agreement, they enter into a subsequent agreement whereby one of the parties is released from his/her obligations under the contract. After the conclusion of that subsequent agreement, the party released will be discharged from further performance of the contract.

2. **Performance**
   A party to a contract may also be discharged by performance. For instance, where a contract is for the performance of specific tasks, once the party concerned completes that task, he has no further performance to render and the contract will automatically come to an end.

3. **Breach**
   As observed above, a breach by one party of a condition of the contract entitles the other party to regard himself as discharged from further performance of the contract. As a result, the latter can terminate the contract and proceed to recover any payment he may have made or any benefit he was supposed to get under the contract.

4. **Frustration**

A party to a contract may also be discharged from further performance by frustration. This type of discharge occurs where a contract that was capable of performance at the time of its conclusion becomes incapable of performance because of subsequent developments.

These developments may be:

- subsequent illegality
- subsequent death of one of the parties
- Subsequent imprisonment of one of the parties for a substantial period of time and
- Subsequent cancellation of an expected event
- The effect of these developments will be to bring the contract to an end forthwith

Remedies

Where the court is satisfied that there has been a breach of contract, it has the power to grant the following remedies:

i. Refusal of further performance by the innocent party. For example, if he has not yet paid the contract price, he can refuse to do so as a result of the party's breach;

ii. Damages as compensation for injury or loss suffered by the innocent party as a result of the breach;

iii. Quantum meruit, i.e. the value of the performance actually rendered by the innocent party.

iv. Specific performance. This remedy allows the innocent party to recover the performance promised by the party in breach and is generally not available except in cases involving land.

Thus, for instance on a breach of the contract for the sale of goods, the court will rarely order the seller to deliver the goods agreed to be sold unless they are unique in some way. Usually in that case it will simply award the innocent party damages representing the value of the good.

In a case where a seller of land fails or refuses to transfer the land to the buyer, the court will order the seller to do the transfer.

v. **Injunction**;

This is an order by the court stopping a contemplated or continuing breach of contract. Of course, this remedy is not final but interim. As a result, it is not uncommon to have an injunction vacated by the court on the application of the party against whom it is granted. Besides an injunction often tends to be for a fixed period of time and will lapse at the expiry of that period unless the court agrees to its extension.

Law of Agency

This is the relation which exists between two persons where one of them has authority or capacity to act on behalf of the other. In other words, agency relation arises whenever one person called the 'Agent' has authority to create legal obligations between the other called the *'principal' and third parties*. Thus, an Agent is only an intermediary between the other called the *'principal' and third parties*.

As a result, although he is bound to exercise his authority in accordance with all the lawful instructions of his principal, an Agent is not (unless he is also an employee of his principal) subject to the direct control or supervision of his principal in the performance of his duties.

Creation of the Agency Relation

The agency relation may be created by the express or implied agreement (which may be but does not need to be contractual) of the principal and the agent.

1. Express Agency

Express agency arises where the principal or some person authorized by him expressly (i.e. in writing or orally) appoints the agent to do either a specified number of things or to act for the principal generally.

2. Implied Agency

Implied agency will arise from the conduct or situation of the parties. And it is immaterial for this purpose that the third person had no authority in fact at the time to enter into that contract for the first person. This is called the doctrine of apparent authority or agency by estoppel

3. Agency by Ratification

Under some circumstances, an act which at the time when it was done lacked authority may by the subsequent conduct of the person on whose behalf lacked authority may by the subsequent conduct of the person on whose behalf lacked authority. For instance, if one person acts in such a way as to lead another person into believing that he has authorized a third person to act on his behalf and that other person in that belief enters into a contract with the third person. The third person will be an agent for the first person in respect of that contract.

This is because the first person is prevented from denying the fact that the person had no authority in fact the third person is his agent. Every act that is not void can be ratified so long as it is capable of ratification by the principal. The illegality of an act does not of itself prevents its ratification. Consequently, a principal may ratify a breach of contract and thus become liable for it

Ratification may be express or may be inferred in appropriate cases even from silence or mere acquiescence. Of course, in that latter case it must be based on the principal's full knowledge of all the essential facts of the act sought to be ratified and must relate to that particular act, and not some other transaction. As a result, the agent will be relieved of personal liability to his principal for acting in excess of his authority and to the third party for possible breach of warranty of authority.

Elements to be present in ratification

(a) The agent must not have been acting for himself in the first place but must have professed to be acting on behalf of a named or ascertainable principal

(b) The principal must have been in existence at the time of the action
This is because a principal who was not in existence at the time when an act was purportedly done on his behalf cannot, on coming into existence, ratify the act

(c) The principal must have been capable of doing the act himself since a person cannot act as an agent for another person who has no capacity to act for himself

(d) The ratification must take place within the time fixed by the transaction itself or within a reasonable time thereafter

Agency by Necessity

The agency relation may also arise by necessity. This will be the case where by reason of an emergency, the relation of principal and agent is deemed to exist between persons who are not otherwise in such a relation. Agency of necessity exists between persons who are not otherwise in such a relation. An agency of necessity exists where to prevent destruction of perishable cargo, a carrier has to take prompt action in excess of his authority and dispose of it.

In other words, as a result of the emergency the agent has to extend his authority to save the principal's property from destruction. For an agency of necessity to arise:

a) The agent should not have been able to communicate with his principal on how to deal with the emergency

b) The action taken should have been necessary in the circumstance in that it was the only reasonable and prudent course open to the agent; and

c) The agent should have acted bona fide in the interests of the parties concerned

Acting in Principle's name

- But regardless of the type of authority involved since an agent derives his authority from his principal, he must act in the principal's name
- However, as will be shown below, the requirement is simply that he must disclose the principal's existence though he may not divulge the principal's identity

Agent's Capacity to Delegate

- An agent cannot delegate his authority except with the principal's express or implied assent
- As a result, in the absence of that assent, the principal will not be bound by the act or contract of a sub-agent whose appointment he has not sanctioned

Agent's Duties to His Principal

- ➤ to perform the act or business undertaken
- ➤ to exercise his discretion. Where the principal does not give him any definition instructions on any particular act or business, the agent must be guided by the honest exercise of his judgment and the principal's interests
- ➤ not to use any materials and information obtained by reason of the agency relation for his personal business
- ➤ to exercise reasonable care, diligence and skill of the principal
- ➤ to avoid any conflict between his interests and those of his principal
- ➤ not to make any secret profit from his position
- ➤ not to deny his principal's rights in an act done or transaction concluded on behalf of the principal

The Agent's Rights against His Principal

- To be paid the agreed remuneration. On the other hand, in the absence of any agreement on the matter, he has no right to be paid anything

- To be reimbursed and indemnified in respect of any expenses or liabilities incurred on behalf of the principal and in the exercise of his authority
- To exercise a right of lien on the principal's goods in respect of all claims against the principal arising out of the agency relation
- If he has bought goods on behalf of the principal with his own money or on credit' he stands towards the principal in the position of an unpaid seller

As a result, on delivery of the goods to a carrier for transmission to the principal, he can stop them in transit and resume possession

Principal's Relations with Third Parties

- Generally, the principal is bound by, and is entitled to the benefit of any contract made by his agent on his behalf within the scope of the agent's authority
- This is so whether at the time of acting the agent name or identified the principal or merely indicated that he was acting for a principal but did not identify him. i.e. the principal was disclosed.
- The rule also applies where the principal is undisclosed. i.e. where he is not known by the third party to be connected with the particular transaction, so long as in entering into the contract the agent clearly indicated that he was not acting on his own behalf.

The Agent's Relations with Third Parties

- A person who makes a contract in his own name without disclosing the existence of any principal is personally liable on the contract to the other contracting even though he may have been acting on behalf of the principal
- Similarly, ifhe claims to act on behalf of another person when the alleged principal does not exist, he will be personally liable for his act
- If he discloses the existence of the principal (ie. Where the principal, is disclosed but is unnamed) or both the existence and identity of

the principal, he will not be subject to personal liability on the contract whether or not he had authority to make the contract

- Of course, where an agent purports to enter into a contract on behalf of a principal when he has no authority, he may be liable to the other party for the breach of warranty of authority unless the principal ratifies the contract

- As observed above, if the contract is ratified, that will have retrospective effect so that the agent's position will be as if he had actual authority to conclude the contract on the principal's behalf when he did so

Termination of Agency

- Just like any other legal relationship between persons, the agency is terminable and that may happen by:

a) express revocation by the principal

b) renunciation by the agent

c) lapse of time. This will be the case where a specific period is fixed for the performance of the act to be done by the agent

d) performance i.e. where the agency was special, after the agent has performed the agreement act so that thereafter he becomes *functus officio*

e) by the death, bankruptcy or insanity of the principal; and the agent; and

f) any act that would generally amount to frustration

Sale of Goods

Contract of Sale of Goods

This is defined as a contract whereby one person (the seller) transfers or agrees to transfer the property in goods to another person (the buyer) for a money consideration called the price. Thus, from this definition it will be clear that the legal objective of the contract of sale of goods is for the buyer to obtain ownership of the goods while the seller receives their price in exchange.

The definition excludes any transaction intended to operate by way of mortgage, pledge, charge or other security. It does not apply to bailment, barter, contract of hire, hire-purchase and contracts for labour and materials. From the statutory definition, it is clear that the following elements must exist in a contract for it to amount to a contract of sale of goods

Buyer and Seller

The buyer is defined as a person who buys or agrees to sell goods. In other words, agreement is not a contract for the sale of goods unless the buyer is bound to buy the goods and the seller is to sell them to him. As a result, where there is a mere option to buy them as under the hire purchase) there will be no account for the sale of goods.

Money Consideration

As definition of a contact of sale of goods it is clear that only contracts under which property in goods is transferred for money will be considered contracts for the sale of goods. On the other hand, a part –exchange transaction in which the agreed price is payable partly in money and

Goods

"Goods" refer to all movable property that is capable of transfer from one person to another by delivery. For the purposes of the contract of sale of goods, goods may be specific, ear marked (i.e. identified by the parties at the time of making the contract) and or unascertained, that is unidentified at the time of the contract and therefore requiring some subsequent agreed act of appropriation by the buyer or seller to earmark them to the contract

Property in Goods

As noted by definition, a contract for sale of goods involves the transfer of property in goods from the seller to the buyer. For this purpose, it would seem that the word "property" refers to the seller's absolute title to goods so that for a person to be able to sell goods under the contract of sale of goods, he must have a right of dominion over them

Form

- There are no legal formalities required for the conclusion of a valid sale of goods

    a)   Passing of Property

- When goods are transferred, the risk of loss or damage to the goods also passes from the seller to the buyer with the transfer of property
- Again, in the event of the seller becoming bankrupt or going into liquidation without having delivered specific goods, the buyer's right to claim possession of the goods from the seller's trustee in bankruptcy or liquidator will depend on whether property in the goods passed to the buyer before the commencement of the bankruptcy or liquidation
- In this case it will be useful to determine the point at which property in goods passes from the seller to the buyer

Specific Goods

Under the law, where there is a sale of specific goods, the property in them will pass to the buyer at such time as the parties intend it to be transferred. And to ascertain that intention, there must be regard to the terms of the contract, the conduct of the parties and the circumstances of the case. Obviously if the parties specifically agree on a particular event e.g. the payment of the price by the buyer or the delivery of the goods to the buyer, then the property will pass on the occurrence of either event.

However, where there is no such agreement or their conduct does not indicate any other intention, property in the goods will pass in accordance to the following rules:

Where the contract of sale is unconditional and the goods are in a deliverable state, property in them will pass to the buyer at the time when the contract is made. Where the seller is bound to do something to the goods to put them in deliverable state, property in them will not pass to the buyer until that is done and the buyer is aware that it has been done. Where the goods are in a deliverable state but the seller has to do something to them to ascertain their price (e.g. weigh, measure or test them) property in them will not pass until that is done and the buyer has noticed that it has been done

Uncertained Goods

Property in this type of goods will not pass until after they have been ascertained, i.e. after they have been unconditionally appropriated to the contract by the seller with the buyer's assent or by the buyer with the seller's assent.

Passing of Risk

Legally the position is that, in the absence of agreement to the contrary by the party's goods remain at the seller's risk until the property in them is transferred to the buyer and once property passes to the buyer, the goods are at his risk even though they may not have been delivered to him.

The word 'risk' is used here in connection with accidental loss or destruction of the goods. As a result, where goods are 'at the seller's risk' this means that if they are accidentally lost without fault on either side, being unable to deliver them to the buyer, the seller cannot recover their price already paid to him in advance. For the same reason, if they are at the buyer's risk and they get accidentally lost, he must pay the price even though he may not have taken possession of them as yet.

In other words, since the risk would be on the buyer, the loss would absolve the seller from his duty to deliver them and the buyer is obliged to accept delivery as if they conformed to the contract.

Transfer of Title

Although the contract of sale of goods is about transfer of property in them to the buyer, it sometimes becomes necessary to deal with the issue of transfer of title. And that question often arises where a non – owner sells the goods and the issue is to determine who, as between their real owner and the buyer is entitled to them.

And the general rule is *nemo dat quod non habet:* the transfer of goods cannot pass a better title than that he himself has. Essentially this means that a buyer of goods from a thief does not get title to them since his seller does not have title in the first place. However, this rule is subject to the following exceptions whose effect is that a person with no title to goods or who has no authority to sell them can pass a good title in them to a third party.

Where the non-owner is an agent of the real owner of the goods and has actual or apparent authority from the latter to sell them. Where the real owner has by his conduct held out the non-owner as being the real owner of the goods. Where the goods are sold on the open market the buyer acquires a good title to them provided he buys them in good faith. Where the seller has a voidable title (where he acquired the goods by misrepresentation, duress or under undue influence) but the title has not been avoided at the time of sale.

Where the goods are sold without the owner's consent by a person exercising statutory power the buyer will get a good title for them.

Implied Obligations in favor of the Buyer

The law imposes a number of obligations on the seller:

- Conditions
- Warranties
- Where the buyer expressly or by implication discloses the purposes for which he requires the goods, it is an implied condition of the contract of sale that the goods will be reasonably suitable for that purpose
- Where there is a sale by sample, it is an implied condition of the contract of sale that the bulk will correspond with the sample in quality

Exclusion Clause

Of course, with the exception of the implied condition relating to the seller's right to sell, all the other implied conditions can be excluded by an appropriately worded clause. The clause must be clear and unambiguous and must be part of the contract of sale of goods.

Performance of the Sale of Goods

In the performance of the contract of sale of goods, the seller and the buyer are under the following mutual obligations:

1. Delivery of the goods to the buyer

    This is the seller's reciprocal duty to the buyer's obligations to accept the goods and pay for them. ***Generally, 'delivery' can be defined as the voluntary transfer of possession of goods from the seller to the buyer.*** Of course, the seller need not physically take the goods to the buyer; it suffices if he makes them available for the buyer to collect them or arrange for their collection.

    In fact, as shown below in the majority of cases the seller delivers goods to the buyer without physically transferring them at all. Delivery may be actual as where the seller transfers physical possession to the buyer or the buyer's agent.

    Delivery may be 'constructive' and not involve any physical transfer of goods at all. Construct delivery may take any one of the following forms:

2. Transfer of a document of title
3. Delivery of an object giving physical control. The delivery to the buyer of keys to premises where the goods are stored is effective delivery of the goods to him
4. Continuous possession. If the buyer was already in possession of the goods as Bailee for the seller before making the contract of sale
5. Delivery to a carrier: where in terms of the contract of sale the seller is authorized or required to send the goods to the buyer, their delivery to the carrier for transmission to the buyer is effective delivery to the buyer

    If the property has already passed to the buyer at the time of rejection, the action may be for damages or for the price of the goods.

Payment for the Goods

The buyer is obliged to pay for the goods in accordance with the terms of the contract of sale.

Remedies for Breach of Contract

Assuming that there has been breach of contract, the following remedies will be available to the parties.

a) Seller

If the property has passed to the buyer and he fails to pay for the goods, the seller can sue him for their price. If the seller is unpaid seller and he still has possession of the goods he can exercise the right of lien on them. The seller also has the right of stoppage of the goods. The unpaid seller also has right to resale the goods and recover from the proceeds of the unpaid price

b) The Buyer

For the buyer he has the following remedies:where the seller fails to comply with any one of the implied conditions, and the condition is not excluded the buyer can reject the goods and refuse to pay for them or recover the price he may have paid for them. As noted above where there is short or excessive delivery or the goods delivered are mixed with non – contract goods buyer is entitled to reject them.

Where the seller wrongfully neglects or refuses to deliver the goods, the buyer is entitled to sue him for breach of contract and recover as damages the estimated loss resulting from that breach. In the case of the seller's wrongful neglect or refusal to deliver the goods the buyer may also be entitled to specific performance

Where the seller is in breach of warranty, or an implied condition but the buyer has accepted the goods so that the breach of condition can only be treated as a breach of warranty, the buyer is entitled to sue him for damages representing the loss resulting from that breach. It should be noted that in the absence of any agreement to the contrary where the buyer refuses to accept goods delivered to him under circumstances where he is entitled to refuse delivery he is not bound to return them to the seller. It suffices to simply intimate to the seller that he refuses to accept them.

Government Regulation

Although most Entrepreneurs recognize the need for some government regulation of business, most believe the process is overwhelming and out of control. Government regulation of business is far from new. To date laws regulating business practices and government agencies to enforce the regulations have expanded continuously.

Most Entrepreneurs agree that some government regulation are necessary. There must be laws governing working safety, environmental protection, package labeling, consumer credit and other relevant issues because some dishonest, unscrupulous managers will abuse the opportunity to serve the public interest.

It is not the regulations that protect workers and consumers and achieve social objectives that businesses object to, but those that produce only marginal benefits relative to their costs. Entrepreneurs especially seek relief from wasteful and meaningless government regulations, charging that the cost of compliance exceeds the benefits gained.

All businesses, regardless of type, must comply with statutes (laws passed by legislative bodies) and regulations (rules enacted by regulatory agencies to carry out the purposes of statutes). These statutes and regulations can come from all levels of government; federal, state, and local. Some of these statutes and regulations apply regardless of the nature of the business and, of course, a venture engaged in business in more than one state or local jurisdiction must comply with applicable laws and regulations from all applicable jurisdictions.

The enforcement agency has no obligation to notify the business that it must comply with the law. It is the business's obligation to inquire and comply. Fortunately, most agencies have public information departments eager to assist in providing information and obtaining compliance. These laws and regulations include licensing and registration of business name, workers compensation, unemployment compensation, and permission to do business in a form other than a sole proprietorship. The collection of sales taxes and the withholding of employees' wages are further examples of obligations with which to comply.

CHAPTER 11

Craft a Winning Business Plan

Let me start by saying your ability to plan and organize every detail of your great business is essential to your success and profitability. A good business plan must contain values: clear ones, core principles: Vision: ideal picture of the future of the business, mission: goals to accomplish, purpose: reasons why business exists, excellent leadership and management, excellent products and services, excellent reputation in market and solid financials.

Crafting a good business plan requires thinking and the quality of your thinking about the key elements of your business has the greatest impact of all on your success and needs you to answer questions like what are the core values and principles that you and your business stand fro and believe in?

If your business was perfect in every way, what would it look like in future? What is your mission for your business defined in terms of how you would want to change or improve the life or work of your customers? Solid business plans don't guarantee success. But for entrepreneurs with decent ideas, they surely boost the odds.

A good plan accomplishes three important tasks. Need-satisfying goods and services which simply put take out marketing there will be no production. Together, production and marketing supply five kinds of economic utility:

- Form Utility Form Utility is provided when someone produces something tangible (things you can touch or see).
- Task Utility Task Utility is provided when someone performs a task for someone else. Thus marketing decisions focus on the customer and include decisions about what goods and services to produce.

  It doesn't make sense to provide goods and services consumers don't want when they are so many things they do want. Marketing is concerned with what customers want – and should guide what is produced and offered. Even when marketing and production combine to provide form or task utility, consumers won't be satisfied until possession, time and place utility are also provided.

- Possession Utility Possession Utility means obtaining a good or service and having the right to use or consume it.
- Time Utility Time Utility means having the product available when the customer wants.
- Place Utility Means having the product available where the customer wants. What are the barriers to entry? Remember to include indirect competitors—those with similar capabilities that currently cater to a different market but could choose to challenge you down the road.

Now that you've established your idea, start addressing the execution—specifically, your team. Include profiles of each of your business's founders, partners or officers and what kinds of skills, qualifications and accomplishments they bring to the table. (Include resumes in an appendix.)

If potential investors have read this far, it's time to give them the nuts and bolts of your business model. This includes a detailed description of all revenue streams (product sales, advertising, services, licensing) and the company's cost structure (salaries, rent, inventory, and maintenance). Be sure to list all assumptions and provide a justification for them.

Also, include names of key suppliers or distribution partners. After all of that, one big question still remains: Exactly how much money does your business stand to make? More important, when will the cash come in the door? That's why you need a section containing past financial performance (if your company is a going concern) and financial projections.

Three-year forward-looking profit-and-loss, balance sheet and cash-flow statements are a must—as is a breakeven analysis that shows how much revenue you need to cover your initial investment. For early stage companies with only so much in the bank, the cash-flow statement comparing quarterly receivables to payables is most critical.

"Everyone misunderstands cash flow," says Tim Berry, president of business-plan software company Palo Alto Software. "People think that if they plan for [accounting] profits, they'll have cash flow. But many companies that go under are profitable when they die, because profits aren't cash."

After you've buffed your plan to a shine, don't file it away First, it aligns the management team toward a common set of goals. Then, once the vision is on paper, it forces the team to take a long, hard look at the feasibility of the business. "A business plan is like a dry run to see if there is a major problem with your business before losing any money," says Mike McKeever, author of "How to Write a Business Plan."

Finally, a business plan is a sales document: It aims to attract professional investors who may only have time for a cursory glance at each idea that crosses their desks. Here, then, are some highlights of an effective business plan. Start with a clear, concise executive summary of your business.

Think of it like an elevator pitch. In no more than two pages, billboard all the important stuff. At the top, communicate your value proposition: what your company does, how it will make money and why customers will want to pay for your product or service. If you are sending your plan to investors, include the amount of money you need and how you plan to use it.

You have to know the whole picture before you can boil things down, so tackle the summary after finishing the rest of your plan. Next, establish the market opportunity. Answer questions like: How large is your target market? How fast is it growing? Where are the opportunities and threats, and how will you deal with them?

Again, highlight your value proposition. Most of this market information can be found through industry associations, chambers of commerce, census data or even from other business owners. (Be sure to source all of your information in case you are asked to back up your claims or need to update your business plan.) While you may have convinced yourself that your product or service is unique, don't fall into that trap.

Instead, get real and size up the competition: Who are they? What do they sell? How much market share do they have? Why will customers choose your product or service instead of buying from your competitors?

Market Strategies

Market strategies are the result of a meticulous market analysis. A market analysis forces the entrepreneur to become familiar with all aspects of the market so that the target market can be defined and the company can be positioned in order to garner its share of sales.

Competitive Analysis

The purpose of the competitive analysis is to determine the strengths and weaknesses of the competitors within your market, strategies that will provide you with a distinct advantage, the barriers that can be developed in order to prevent competition from entering your market, and any weaknesses that can be exploited within the product development cycle.

Design and the Development Plan

The purpose of the design and development plan section is to provide investors with a description of the product's design, chart its development within the context of production, marketing and the company itself, and create a development budget that will enable the company to reach its goals.

Operations and Management Plan

The operations and management plan is designed to describe just how the business functions on a continuing basis. The operations plan will highlight the logistics of the organization such as the various responsibilities of the management team, the tasks assigned to each division within the company, and capital and expense requirements related to the operations of the business.

Financial Factors Financial data is always at the back of the business plan, to gather dust. "A business plan is the beginning of a process," says Berry. "Planning is like steering, and steering means constantly correcting errors. The plan itself holds just a piece of the value; it's the going back and seeing where you were wrong and why that matters."

Further, before coming up with a winning business plan you need to ask yourself the following questions: How long should the business plan be? When should you write it? Who needs a business plan? Why should you write a business plan? After answering these questions you need to determine your goals and objectives, outline your financing needs, plan what you'll do with your plan and of course don't forget about marketing.

A great business plan should consist of the following sections: Executive Summary Within the overall outline of the business plan, the executive summary will follow the title page. The summary should tell the reader what you want. This is very important.

All too often, what the business owner desires is buried on page eight. Clearly state what you're asking for in the summary.

Business Description

The business description usually begins with a short description of the industry. When describing the industry, discuss the present outlook as well as future possibilities. You should also provide information on all the various markets within the industry, including any new products or developments that will benefit or adversely affect your business.

Nothing stifles implementation like unrealistic goals. 4. Is the plan complete? Does it include all the necessary elements? Requirements of a business plan vary, depending on the context. There is no guarantee, however, that the plan will work if it doesn't cover the main bases.

Too many people think of business plans as something you do to start a company, apply for a loan, or find investors. Yes, they are vital for those purposes, but there's a lot more to it. Preparing a business plan is an organized, logical way to look at all of the important aspects of a business.

First, decide what you will use the plan for, such as to: • Define and fix objectives, and programs to achieve those objectives.

• Create regular business review and course correction.

• Define a new business. • Support a loan application. • Define agreements between partners.

• Set a value on a business for sale or legal purposes. • Evaluate a new product line, promotion, or expansion. No time to plan?

A common misconception "Not enough time for a plan," business people say. "I can't plan. I'm too busy getting things done." A business plan now can save time and stress later. Too many businesses make business plans only when they have to. Unless a bank or investors want to look at a business plan, there isn't likely to be a plan written.

The busier you are, the more you need to plan. If you are always putting out fires, you should build fire breaks or a sprinkler system. You can lose the whole forest for too much attention to the individual trees. but that doesn't mean it's any less important than up-front material such as the business concept and the management team.

What makes a good Business Plan?

What factors are involved in creating a good business plan? Is it the length of the plan? The information it covers? How well it is written or the brilliance of its strategy. The following illustration shows a business plan as part of a process.

You can think about the good or bad of a plan as the plan itself, measuring its value by its contents. There are some qualities in a plan that make it more likely to create results, and these are important. However, it is even better to see the plan as part of the whole process of results, because even a great plan is wasted if nobody follows it.

A business plan will be hard to implement unless it is simple, specific, realistic and complete. Even if it is all these things, a good plan will need someone to follow up and check on it. The plan depends on the human elements around it, particularly the process of commitment and involvement, and the tracking and follow-up that comes afterward.

Successful implementation starts with a good plan. There are elements that will make a plan more likely to be successfully implemented. Some of the clues to implementation include:

1. Is the plan simple? Is it easy to understand and to act on? Does it communicate its contents easily and practically?

2. Is the plan specific? Are its objectives concrete and measurable? Does it include specific actions and activities, each with specific date of completion, specific persons responsible and specific budgets?
3. Is the plan realistic? Are the sales goals, expense budgets realistic?
4. Planning is a guide to implementation and control. Marketing plan fills out marketing strategy.

Keys to Better Business Plans

The following keys constitute better business plans:

1. Use a business plan to set concrete goals, responsibilities, and deadlines to guide your business.
2. A good business plan assigns tasks to people or departments and sets milestones and deadlines for tracking implementation.
3. A practical business plan includes 10 parts implementation for every one part strategy.
4. As part of the implementation of a business plan, it should provide a forum for regular review and course corrections.
5. Good business plans are practical.
6. Don't use a business plan to show how much you know about your business.
7. Nobody reads a long-winded business plan: not bankers, bosses, nor venture capitalists. Years ago, people were favorably impressed by long plans. Today, nobody is interested in a business plan more than 50 pages long. 10 to 15 pages is fine.

PART THREE

TOTAL BUSINESS MASTERY

CHAPTER 12

Design a Great Product or Service

The quality of your product or service determines 90% of business success. Quality is the key determinate of your growth and profitability. It is determinate of your reputation. How often customers say: "This is a great product or service!"

To this end you need to decide what exactly you intend to sell. Some questions include: what does your customer consider value and is willing to pay for it? What will be the best compliments that you receive from your happy customer? What will your products offer to your customers that make them superior to your competitors? What will your products or services offer to your customers that will make them superior to your competitors? What products or services should you abandon or discontinue because you cannot achieve excellence in those areas? The market only rewards for excellent products and services.

Although production is a necessary economic activity, some people overrate its importance in relation to marketing. Production and marketing are both important parts of a total business system aimed at providing consumers with need-satisfying goods and services. Simply put, take out marketing there will be no production. Together, production and marketing supply five kinds of economic utility:

- Form Utility

Form Utility is provided when someone produces something tangible (things you can touch or see).

- Task Utility

Task Utility is provided when someone performs a task for someone else. Thus, marketing decisions focus on the customer and include decisions about what goods and services to produce. It doesnot make sense to provide goods and services consumers donot want when they are so many things that they want.

Marketing is concerned with what customers want – and should guide what is produced and offered. Even when marketing and production are combined to provide form or task utility, consumers can not be satisfied until possession, time and place utility are also provided.

- Possession Utility

Possession Utility means obtaining goods or services and having the right to use or consume them.

- Time Utility

Time Utility means having the product available WHEN the customer wants.

- Place Utility

This Means having the product available WHERE the customer wants.

CHAPTER 13

Strategic Analysis

A successful external analysis needs to be directed and purposeful. The external analysis process should not be an end in itself. Rather, it should be motivated throughout by a desire to effect strategy, to generate or evaluate strategic options. The investment decision, where to compete, involves questions such as:

- Should existing business areas be liquidated, milked, maintained or invested for growth?
- What growth directions should receive investment?
- Should there be market penetration, product expansion or market expansion
- Should new business areas be entered?

When Should External Analysis Be Conducted?

There is often a tendency to relegate the external analysis to an annual exercise. The annual planning cycle can provide a stimulus to review and change strategies that can be health. However, a substantial risk exists in maintaining external analysis as once – a year event. Thus the need for strategic review and change is often continuous. Information sensing and analysis therefore need to be continuous. External analysis deliberately commences with customer and competitor analyses.

Customer Analysis

In most strategic market – planning contexts, the first logical step is to analyze customers. Customer analysis starts with segmentation.

1. Segmentation

   - Who are the biggest customers?
   - The most profitable
   - The most attractive potential customers
   - Do the customers fall into any logical groups on the base of needs, motivations or characteristics?
   - How should the market be segmented into groups that would require a unique business strategy?

2. **Customer Motivation or Customer Behaviour**

   - This looks at questions such as:
   - Why do customers select and use their favorite brands?
   - What elements of the product/service do they value most?
   - What are the customers' objectives?
   - What are they really buying?
   - What changes are occurring in customer motivation?
   - What motivates them to go to supplier x or y?
   - Customer analysis is trying to be close as possible to them to know what motivates them to go to supplier x

As entrepreneurs we need to convince them that they have been going to wrong products but they should have come to us. It is up to us to convince them that our product, price, place (channels of distribution) and promotional methods will be able to bring solutions to their problems. The idea is feedback and making sure that they always comeback (Customer Relationship Marketing). Always be ahead of customers with new ideas (4Ps).

3. **The Unmet Needs**

   - Why are some customers dissatisfied?
   - What are the unmet needs that customers can identify?
   - Do these unmet needs represent leverage points for competitors

Competitor Analysis

- On competitor analysis marketing managers need to analyse the following:

  ✓ Current and Past Strategies
  ✓ Organizational Culture
  ✓ Cost Structures
  ✓ The Marketing Objectives
  ✓ Size, growth and profitability
  ✓ Exit barriers
  ✓ Strengths and weaknesses

Marketing Analysis

In marketing analysis marketing entrepreneurs need to analyze the following:

➢ Actual and potential size of the market
➢ Analyse Competitors
➢ Analyse Target Market (Size of Customers)
➢ Mission (In what Business are we in?) – otherwise you will be analyzing wrong markets
➢ Market Growth (Use the Product Life Cycle)
➢ Demand (Go to Markets that are more demanded).
➢ Go to attractive markets
➢ Cost structure in the market
➢ Market Mix Variables (Product, Price, Place and Promotion Decisions)
➢ Marketing Trends (Customer Behaviour, Revenue – Big Customers)
➢ Build Capacity (Capacity Management) -
➢ technology,
➢ Skills (Staffing with Right Skills)
➢ Organizational capabilities,
➢ Assets among others

CHAPTER 14

Craft a Great Marketing Plan

Market planning is a guide to implementation and control. Marketing plan fills out marketing strategy. A market strategy sets a target market and a marketing mix. So a marketing plan is a written statement of a marketing strategy and the time related details for carrying out the strategy.

Thus the marketing plan should spell out: What marketing mix will be offered; to whom (the target market) and for how long? What company resources will be needed at what rate, the plan should also include some control procedures. After the marketing plan is developed, a marketing manager knows what needs to be done. The marketing manager is concerned with implementation – putting marketing plans into operation, Control is simply analyzing and correcting what you have done

All business strategy is marketing strategy. Your ability to attract qualified prospects determines your success in business. This means that you are responsible for making critical strategic decisions for your business.

Additionally, Market Strategy Planning means finding attractive opportunities and developing profitable marketing strategies. A market strategy specifies a target market and a related marketing mix. A target market is a fairly homogeneous (similar) group of customers to whom a company wishes to appeal. A market mix is the controllable variables the company puts together to satisfy this target group (Product, Price, Promotion and Place).

The Marketing Plan Model

Source: Author (2020)

Mission Statement

This is a description of what the business intends to do to its costomers. Customers are the perceived to be reasons why the business exists. Usually a good mission statement answers questions such as in what business are we in? why are we in business? What products and services are we going to produce and what markets are we going to target?

Marketing Objectives

These are yardstics to measure the departmental performance of the business. Marketing objectives include but not limited to: increasing the market share; maximizing revenue, continuity of profits, increasing cashflow and business growth.

Situation Analysis

As we have seen a marketing orientation begins and ends with the customer. Thus analysis in marketing management involves finding the answers to the following questions:

- ✓ Who are our customers and potential customers?
- ✓ Who do they buy (or not buy)
- ✓ Do they buy our product or service?
- ✓ When do they buy it?
- ✓ Where do they buy it?
- ✓ How do they buy it?
- ✓ Having bought the product are they satisfied with it?
- ✓ How are customer needs changing?
- ✓ Which of the competitor's products do they consider buying?

Marketing Strategy

Market Strategy Planning means finding attractive opportunities and developing profitable marketing strategies. Marketing Strategy what is it? A market strategy specifies a target market and a related marketing mix. A target market is a fairly homogeneous (similar) group of customers to whom a company wishes to appeal.

A market mix – the controllable variables the company puts together to satisfy this target group (Product, Price, Promotion and Place). The effective use of the marketing tools within the marketing mix is an interrelated manner and is the key to successful marketing and to a profitable business.

Therefore the aim of marketing management is to get quality to the right place at the right price, using the right promotional methods. After the marketing plan is developed, a marketing manager knows what needs to be done. The entrepreneur is concerned with implementation – putting marketing plans into operation.

Strategy Implementation

Without focusing on implementation it will be just a mere thinking on paper. Translating strategy into action is concerned with ensuring that strategies are working in practice. Implementation of strategy involves formulating budgets, programmes, looking at staffing, skills and structure issues among others.

Strategy implemntation is therefore concerned with exploiting the strategic capability of an organization in terms of resources and competencies. The idea is to provide a competitive advantage and yield new opportunities.

Evaluation and Control

Control is simply analyzing and correcting what you have done. This involves checking results whether the objectives are met. Corrective actions are made based on variances or standard deviations.

The effective use of the marketing tools within the marketing mix is an interrelated manner and is the key to successful marketing and to a profitable business. Therefore the aim of marketing management is to get quality to the right place at the right price, using the right promotional methods

Your competition determines your level of sales, the prices you charge and how much money you make. Your decisions in these areas determine the success or failure of your business. This leads to four key marketing principles: specialization, differentiation, segmentation and concentration:-

- **Specialization:** This is the product, service, customer, market, area of technology where you focus all your efforts.
- **Differentiation:** This is your competitive advantage, your area of excellence and superiority, your unique selling position.

- **Segmentation:** You will need to find out who are those customers who most appreciate your area of superiority.
- **Concentration:** This where you focus the best possible ways to contact your ideal customers. You also need to decide on the best media and what the most powerful appeals are. A great Marketing Plan therefore attracts a steady stream of qualified prospects. Market Plan emphasizes your Unique Selling Position and positions your product as the first best choice in the customers' mind.
- **Strategy Preeminence:** Your goal is to position yourself in your market as the only choice for what you sell. The Marketing Plan thus will help your business define and specify marketing efforts to maximize marketing resources and to increase revenue. You need to customize the marketing strategy, marketing budget, direct competitors, barriers to market entry, and more. By investing a few minutes in this chapter, your business will have a thorough Marketing Plan that will hone marketing efforts and maximize revenue.

Elements of A Good Marketing Plan

1. Situation Analysis

   a. External Environment

   - Regulatory
   - Political
   - Economic
   - Social
   - International

   b. Corporate Review

   - Mission statement, Corporate vision, strategic intent
   - Corporate plan
   - Long term goals
   - Objectives such as profit, ROI, share price
   - Organizational chart

c. Product Category Review

General description (life cycle state, needs/want specified). Sales trends (years, seasonality, share of major brands)

- Distribution profile
- Pricing overview
- Packaging overview

d. Competitive Analysis
Description of major competitors' strength/weakness

i.   Product
ii. Distribution
iii. Pricing

Brand positioning and advertising

i.   Media spending (by medium, seasonality)
ii. sales promotion (trade vs. consumer)
     Anticipated major programs (brands, new territo- ries, changes in distribution, pricing, marketing comunication)

e. Consumer Analysis

- Customers/buyers vs. consumers/users (& influences)
- Demographics and psychographics
- Purchase rate
- Brand loyalty analysis
- Difference between brand and category users

f. Brand Review

g. Current positioning, sales trends, performance test results, awareness, pricing history, distribution history marketing communication history, stage in brand life cycle, source of additional business.

CHAPTER 15

Business Growth Strategies

Figure below presents the traditional life- cycle stages of an enterprise. These stages include new venture development, start-up activities, growth, stabilization, and innovation or decline.

Figure 15:1 Venture Growth Stages

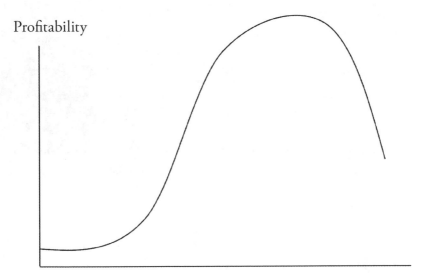

Profitability

Revenue

New-Venture Venture Business Innovation
Start-up Growth Stabilization or Decline

Source: Ngwira (2015), Development Activities

New venture development

The first stage, new venture development, consists of activities associated with the initial formulation of the venture. This initial phase is the foundation of entrepreneurial process and requires creativity and assessment.

In addition to the accumulation and expansion of resources, this is a creativity, assessment, and networking stage for initial for initial entrepreneurial strategy formulation. Thus, the enterprise general philosophy, mission, scope and direction are determined during this stage.

Startup activities

The second stage, startup activities, encompasses the foundation work for creating a formal business plan, searching for capital, carrying out market activities and developing an effective entrepreneurial team. These activities typically demand an aggressive entrepreneurial strategy with maximum efforts devoted to launching the venture. This stage is similar to chandler's description of rationalization of the use of the firm's resources. Strategic and operational planning steps designed to identify the firm's competitive advantage and operational planning steps designed to identify it. Many business managers say that marketing and financial considerations tend to be paramount during this stage.

Growth

The growth stage often requires major changes in entrepreneurial strategy. Competition and other marketing forces call for the reformation of strategies. For example, some firms find themselves "growing out" of business because they are unable to cope with the growth of their ventures. Many business commentators say that highly creative Entrepreneurs sometimes are unable, or unwilling, to meet the administrative challenges that accompany this growth stage.

As a result, they leave the ventures and move on to other ventures. The creative ideas are detrimental to the growth of the venture. The firm needed a managerial Entrepreneur to run the operations: jobs had neither the expertise nor the desire to assume this role.

The growth stage presents newer and more substantial problems than those the Entrepreneur faced during the startup stage. These newer challenges force the entrepreneur into developing step of skills while maintaining an "entrepreneurial perspective" for the organization. Thus, the growth stage is a transition from entrepreneurial one-person leadership to managerial team-oriented leadership.

Business Stabilization

Business commentators say that the stabilization stage is a result of both marketing conditions and the entrepreneur's efforts. During this stage a number of developments commonly occur, including increased competition, consumer difference to the Entrepreneur's good(s) or service(s) and situation of the market with a host of "me too" looks-likes.

Thus, sales often begin to stabilize and Entrepreneur begins thinking about where the enterprise will go over the next three years. Many writers describe this stage as a swing stage in that it proceeds the period when the firm either swings into higher gear and greater profitability of swings toward decline and failure. During this stage innovations is often critical to future success.

Innovation or Decline

Generally, firms that fail to innovate will die. Financially successful enterprises often will try to acquire other innovative firms, thereby ensuring their own growth. Also, many firms will work on new products/services development.

Why so many businesses fail

According to longitudinal study conducted by Jones (2005), approximately 60% of small businesses shut down within the first six years.

Small businesses fail to grow for numerous reasons. The most common reasons are: because their owners: grow their company too fast: have a poor concept: are not good at marketing or sales: fail to plan: start their company without enough money to get to breakeven: have an inability to differentiate: lack control of their finances and books: or donot build systems and processes. Many entrepreneurs who end their finances and books: or donot build systems and processes. Many Entrepreneurs who end up unsuccessful do not build process and systems and lack the ability or desire to sell.

They do not carefully plan their business and often fail to raise the needed capital to sustain it until it is profitable. They do not focus on efficiency of operations or automation. They make the investment in additional capital or employees needed to expand the company to the point where it can make profit. As an Entrepreneur, even if you have a great idea, you will have to plan well, build a long-term team, make sure you have adequate capitalization, build the proper systems, and execute your plan.

According to Entrepreneur and adjunct business professor at UNC's Kenan-Flagler Business School Colin Wahl, there are certain critical success factors in building a successful small business. These include: vision of the management: passion: a good idea: clean, focused business objectives: a well thought through business plan: good organization:enthusiasm in the owners: a good team: motivated employees: good cash flow management: adequate financial resources: a clear understanding of marketing need: and execution of the management.

The different routes to growth are follows:

Organic Growth

This occurs when a business grows by using its existing resources. Organic growth can take place because the market is growing, or because the business organization is doing increasingly better than its competitors or is entering new markets. Exploiting a product advantage can sustain organic growth. Organic growth depends on a firm's available resources and capabilities as well as its planning, time and cash.

Mergers and Acquisitions

One of the fastest routes to growth is through an acquisition or merger, but it is one of the hardest and riskiest. There are two views about mergers. One is that mergers between titans will result in an even larger titan, too cumbersome to operate as flexibly and efficiently as it needs to. According to this view a merger results in more bureaucracy, diminishing returns negating the benefits of increases in size and capacity for production, diseconomies of scale, swallowing huge quantities of capital and causing organizational lethargy; and a lumbering giant that will be outpaced and outsmarted by smaller rivals.

The second, more optimistic, view is that mergers result in: economies of scale and efficiency; stability and greater potential for growth resulting from a broader base of customers and products; and an intellectual capital and management infrastructure to deal with market change.

Specialization

The opposite of diversification, specialization involves dropping non-core activities, or even redefining and focusing on core operations. The main advantages are clear focus and strength in depth, with all available resources channeled into one endeavour. It also means that any cash available from the sale of non-core operations can be used to grow on the business. Reliance on specialization requires doing what you do sufficiently better than your competitors and successfully anticipating and adapting to market changes.

Competitive Advantage

When a firm sustains profit that exist the average of its industry, the firm is said to possess a competitive advantage over its rivals. The goal of much of business strategy is to achieve a sustainable competitive advantage. Michael Porter identified two basic types of competitive advantage: cost advantage and differentiation.

A competitive advantage exists when the firm is able to deliver the same benefits as competitors but at lowest cost (cost advantage), or deliver benefits that exceed those of competing products (differentiation advantage). Thus a competitive advantage enables the firm to create superior value for its customers and superior profits for itself.

Cost and differentiation advantages are known as position advantages since they describe the firm's position in the industry as a leader in either cost or differentiation. A resource based view emphasizes that a firm utilizes its resources and capabilities to create a competitive advantage that ultimately results in superior value creation.

Managing Industry Competition

The slow economic growth rates that have characterised many industries in recent years have given way to zero – sum markets. A company can therefore only grow by beating others. This calls for strong competitor's strategy. Maintenance of a strong and successful market position or the achievement of rapid growth usually reflects a strong and successful competitor strategy. The converse to this statement is that rapid decline and weakening of business position reflects a poor competitor strategy.

Segmentation Strategy

What is market segmentation?: Is a relatively homogeneous group of customers who will respond to a marketing mix in a similar way. Market segmentation is a two way process: naming broad product markets and segmenting those broad markets in order to select target markets and develop suitable marketing mixes.

A good market segmentation should have the following characteristics: homogeneous (similar) customers in a segment should be as similar as possible with respect to their behaviour and likely responses, heterogeneous (different) customers in different segments should be as different as possible with respect to their likely responses, substantial - the segment should be big enough to be profitable, operational - the segmenting dimensions should be useful for identifying customers and deciding on marketing mix variables.

Reasons for segmentation include: to understand the customers, to focus activities, to reduce risks, to defeat the competitors and to assist in planning. There are three ways to develop market oriented strategies in a broad product market. The single target market approach - segmenting the market and picking one of the homogeneous segments as the firm's target market, the multiple target approach -segmenting the market and choosing two or more segments then treating each as a separate target market needing a different marketing mix and the combined target market approach - combining two or more submarkets into one larger market as a basis for one strategy.

All these three approaches involve target marketing. (1) and (2) are called segmenters and (3) are called combiners. They try to increase the size of their target market by combining two or more segments. Segmenters aim at one or more homogeneous segments.

They try to develop a different marketing mix for each segment. Segmenters usually adjust their market mixes for each target market. Segmenters believe that aiming at one or some of these smaller markets makes it possible to satisfy the target customers better and provide greater profit potential for the firm.

These include geographical, behavioural and demographic characteristics, qualifying dimensions are those relevant to including a customer type in a product market. While determining dimensions include those that actually affect the customer's purchase of a specific product or brand in a product market. Cluster analysis and positioning are a more sophisticated computer aided techniques of segmenting the market. It involves finding similar patterns within sets of data. Focusing on target markets helps one to fine tune the marketing mix.

Positioning

This is another approach which helps identify product market opportunities. Positioning shows how customers locate proposed or present brands in market. It entails some formal marketing research. Managers should decide whether to leave the product (and marketing mix) alone or reposition it e.g. an advert.

This may mean physical changes in the product or simply image changes based on promotion. Firms often use promotion to help "position" how a product meets a target market's specific needs. Positioning helps managers understand how customers see their market. This is called "perceptual mapping".

Bcg Growth – Share Matrix

Businesses that are big enough to be organized into strategic business units face the challenge of allocating resources among those units. Boston Consulting Group developed a model for managing a portfolio of different business units (or major product lines).

15.2 Experience Curve

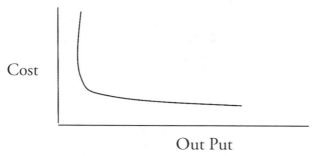

Cost

Out Put

Source : Author (2020)

The premises of the BCG findings are these: That in any market segment of an industry price level tend to be very similar for products. Therefore what makes one company more profitable than the rest must be the levels of its costs. It is the key determinants of low cost levels that the BCG attempted to unearth. Their arguments can be summarised as follows:

Total Units Produced

The relationship between unit costs and total costs produced over time. Significant cost is a function of experience and then cost is a function of a market share. Market share does not necessary relate to the overall market. The overall implications of BCG's findings are that successful companies make almost all their profits from products in which they dominate their market segment. This view has become a very strong influence on many company's choices of strategy

Product Portfolio

In order to dominate a market a company must normally gain that dominance when the market is in growth stage of the product life cycle. In a state of maturity a market is likely to be stable with customer loyalties fairly fixed. It is therefore more difficult to gain share. The BCG has suggested the model of the product portfolio or the growth share matrix as a tool by which to consider product strategy. The matrix combines market growth rate and market share and thus directly relates to the idea of the experience curve.

The BCG growth – share matrix displays the various business units on a graph of the market rate vs. market share relative to competitors:

Fig 15:3 BCG Growth - Share Matrix

		Market Share	
		High	Low
Market Growth	High	Stars	Question Marks
	Low	Cash Cow	Dog

Source : Boston Consulting Group

Resources are allocated to business units according to where they are situated as follows:

A question mark (or problem child) is in a growing market but does not have a high market share. Its parent company may be spending heavily to increase the market share

A star is a product (or business) which has a high market share in a growing market. The business is able to break even and make profits though it spends heavily to increase the market share

A cash cow is a product (or business) with high market share in a mature market. Because growth is low and market conditions are more stable the need for heavy marketing investment is less. The cash cow is thus a cash provider

Dogs have a low market share and low market growth. They are cash drain

To portray alternative corporate growth strategies, Igor Ansoff presented a matrix that focused on the firm's present and potential product and markets (customers). By considering ways to grow via existing products and new products, and in existing markets and new markets, there are four possible product-market combinations.

Fig. 15.4 Ansoff Matrix

	Existing Products	**New Products**
Existing Markets	Market Penetration	Product Development
New Markets	Marketing Development	Diversification

Market Penetration – the firm seeks to achieve growth with existing products in the current market segments, aiming to increase its market share.

Market Development – the firm seeks growth by targeting its existing products to new market segments.

Product Development – the firm develops new products targeted to its existing market segments.

Diversification- the firm grows into new businesses by developing new products for new markets.

Resource Based View Strategy

Organizations are dynamic entities, linking the activities through a set of connections that can be both complex and simple. Emphasizing one aspect or resource in the business has profound implications for the rest of the organization. Understanding how to assess and manage this web of interactions lies at the heart of systems thinking and is central to developing a flexible and robust strategy and then implementing it successfully.

Kim Warren, a management writer, highlights the fact that possibly the greatest challenge facing managers is to understand how to build their business's performance over both the short and long term. When the causes of performance through time are not understood companies tend to make poor choices about their future. They embark upon plans they cannot achieve, failing to assemble what they need. This is called critical path the journey the business takes in seeking to improve its performance and value.

Strategies for Managing Industry Competition

Doyle (2002) observes that the slow economic growth rates that have characterised many industries in recent years have given way to zero – sum markets. A company can therefore only grow by beating others. Thos calls for a strong competitor's strategy. Aaker (2001) states that maintenance of a strong market position or the achievement of rapid growth usually reflects a strong and success competitor strategy. The converse ti this statement is that rapid decline and weakening of business positions reflects a poor competitor strategy. Whether this is true for the case of SMEs in Malawi is open to argument.

D'Aven (2002) argues that when established companies do succumb to a revolution, they usually have only themselves to blame. Either they have ignored the threat for too long. Or they have hyperactively embraced it too quickly, wasting their resources and destroying their existing strengths without acquiring new ones.

These arguments stipulate that a careful understanding of the right response to competitor activity as well as achieving the business objective of long – term survival, growth and profitability. This literature on competition strategies insights into the business competitive environment and deserves lessons for achieving improved performance through employment of successful competitor strategies.

Wilson (1999) observes that increasingly, competition is not between individual companies, but rather between whole networks – with the prize going to the company that has built better network. The operating principle is simple: build a good network of relationships with key stakeholders and profits will follow. Christopher (2001) puts more emphasis to this school of bought by stating that in today's market, "supply chain now competes against another supply chain" (Christopher, 2001, pp 22). This calls for competing players in a market to look beyond their direct competitors and start search for strategic competitive advantages across the whole range of the supply chain in which they are involved.

Growth Strategies for Hostile and Declining Markets

Declining markets as well as mature markets can present real opportunities for a business following the right strategy. As such declining markets are not to be always avoided. Businesses that view an industry's decline as an opportunity rather than just a problem and make objective decisions can reap handsome rewards.

A firm can try to increase its market share further, even if market size remains constant. These views suggest that it may not always be the best option to pull out of a market whenever the environment does not look promising. With the right strategies in place, it is possible to turn around performance in such challenging market environments.

CHAPTER 16

Ethics in Business

Many Business Commentators say that business ethics is critical and is a structured examination of how people and institutions should behave in the world of commerce. In particular, it involves examining appropriate constraints on the pursuit of self-interest, or (for firms) profits, when the actions of individuals or firms affect others. At the heart of business ethics is rightness or wrongness. For example, is it morally right to engage in insider trading? Is it morally correct to be involved in corporate lies? However, many business commentators say that business ethics is the discipline of applying general ethical dilemmas in business dealings.

The rule of the game is that you need to be smart. Never use shortcut suicide. As professional entrepreneur ensure that you are not involved in anything illegal. In simple terms do not indulge yourself in anything that is ethically questionable.

According to Chris (2009) *"BUSINESS ETHICS" is the study of ethical dilemmas, values, and decision-making in the world of commerce.* It applies to all aspects of business conduct and is relevant to the conduct of individuals and business organizations as a whole. Business ethics (also known as Corporate ethics) is a form of professional ethics that examines ethical principles and moral or ethical problems that arise in a business environment.

Applied ethics is a field of ethics that deals with ethical questions in many fields such as medical, technical, legal and business ethics. Business ethics can be both a normative and a descriptive discipline. As a corporate practice and a career specialization, the field is primarily normative. In academia descriptive approaches are also taken. The range and quantity of business ethical issues reflects the degree to which business is perceived to be at odds with non-economic social values.

Business ethics and the changing Environment

Businesses and governments operate in changing technological, legal, economic, social and political environments with competing stakeholders and power claims. Stakeholders are individuals, companies, groups and nations that cause and respond to: external issues, opportunities and threats. Internet and information technologies, globalization, deregulation, mergers and wars, have accelerated rate of change and uncertainty.

In today's dynamic and complex environment stakeholders such as professionals, shareholders, management, employees, consumers, suppliers and members of community must make and manage business and moral decisions.

Environmental Forces and Stakeholders Organizations are embedded in and interact with multiple changing local, national and international environments. These environments are increasingly moving toward and emerging into a global system of dynamically interrelated interactions among local, national and international.

A first step toward understanding stakeholder issues is to gain an understanding of environmental forces that influence issues and stakes of different groups. This is a call to think globally before acting locally in many situations. As we discuss an overview of these environmental forces here, think of the effects and pressures each of the forces has on your industry, company, profession or career and job.

Stakeholder Management Approach

The question is: how do companies, communication media, political groups, consumers, employees, competitors and other groups respond when they are affected by an issue, dilemma, threat or opportunity from one or more of the environments described? The stakeholder management approach is a way of understanding the effects of environmental forces and groups on specific issues that affect real – time stakeholders and their welfare.

The stakeholder approach begins to address these questions by enabling individuals and groups to articulate collaborative, win – win strategies. The underlying aim here is to develop awareness of the ethics and social responsibility of different stakeholders' perceptions, plans, strategies and actions.

Business Ethics: Why Does It Matter?

Business ethicists ask, "What is right and wrong, good and bad, and harmful and beneficial regarding decisions and actions in and around organizational activities? Ethical "solutions" to business and organizational problems may seem available. Thus, learning to think, reason and act ethically can enable us to first be aware and recognize a potential problem.

"Doing the right thing" matters to all stakeholders.

To companies and employers, acting legally and ethically means saving billions of dollars each year in lawsuits, settlements and theft. Studies have also shown that corporations also have paid significant financial penalties for acting unethically. *Costs to businesses also include: deterioration of relationships; damage to reputation; declining employee productivity; loyalty and absenteeism; companies that have a reputation of unethical and uncaring behavior toward employees also have a difficult time recruiting and retaining valued professional.*

For business leaders and managers, managing ethically also means managing with integrity. Integrity cascades throughout an organization. It shapes and influences the values, tone and culture of the organization, commitment and imagination of everyone in a company. Then, we can evaluate our own and other's values, assumptions and judgments regarding the problem before we act.

Laura Nash points out that business ethics deals with three basic areas of managerial decisions making. First, is a choice about what the laws should be and whether to follow them. Second, choices about economic and social issues outside the domain of law, and lastly, choices about the priority of self – interest over the company's interest.

What Are Unethical Business Practices? Surveys identify prominent everyday ethical issues facing businesses and their stakeholders. Recurring themes include: managers lying to employees or vice versa; office favoritism; taking credit for others' work; receiving or offering kickbacks; stealing from the company; firing an employee for whistle-blowing. padding expenses accounts to obtain reimbursements for questionable business expenses; divulging confidential information or trade secrets commonly called insider trading; terminating employment without giving sufficient notice and using company property and materials for personal use.

Things That Ethics Promotes

- Openness and transparency
- Honesty and integrity
- Excellence and quality
- Public accountability
- Legality
- Promote justice
- Confidential information
- Balanced decisions
- Whistle blowing

Relativism

Although relativism is most often associated with ethics, one can find defenses of relativism in virtually any area of philosophy. Both relativism and morality involve the field of ethics, also called moral philosophy, which involves systematic, defending and recommending concepts of right and wrong behavior. ***The term ethics is also defined as a discipline involving inquiry into more judgments people make and the rules and principles upon which such judgments are based.***

There are two different versions of relativism: Factual Moral Relativism (FMR) and Normative Ethical Relativism (NER) as it is often claimed that moral beliefs are in fact relative. It will be useful to generalize a distinction familiar from discussions of ethical relativism and to distinguish FMR and NER with respect to anything that is claimed to be relative.

Moral beliefs are in fact relative, that different people do make different moral judgments and advocates different more rules and principles. Thus, FMR claims that moral ideals and the like are often countered by arguments that such things are universal. Therefore, FMR are empirical claims that may tempt us to conclude that they are little philosophical interests, but there are several reasons why this is so.

This position is called FMR and as factual matter, the truth of FMR can be decided by empirical investigation. On the other hand, Normative Ethical Relativism (NER) is a claim that an Act in Society S is right if and only if most people in society S believe A is right. This is a Universal Normative Principal in so far as it applies to any person in society.

However, the possibility of NER arises only when some action or practice is the focus of disagreement between holders of two self-contained and exclusive systems. For example, two systems of beliefs, S1 and S2, are exclusive of one another when they have consequences that disagree under some description but do not require either to abandon their side of the disagreement.

Thus, a real confrontation between S1 and S2 would occur when S2 is real option for the group living under S1. From the forgoing discussion we can conclude that NER seems to be a less powerful tool not robust enough and less convincing since in both society S1 and fails to understand why the same tool is interpreted differently.

However, it is argued that if the principal of tolerance is accepted the society groups need not impose nor foster tolerance on moral beliefs on others. On such, NER can be accepted because it is the only normative principal with commitment to tolerance. To their concepts, beliefs or modes of reasoning, then groups cannot differ with respect to their concepts, beliefs or modes of reasoning.

Further, the NER supported by FMR takes on a more practical task, which is to arrive on one hand. FMR does not necessarily deny the existence of a single correct moral appraisal, given the same set of circumstances. This means that FMR as a tool for supporting NER with empirical investigation NER in a given area tends to counsel tolerance of practices that conform to alternatives standards prevailing in the area. FMR input into NER claims that different cultures have different views of morality, which they unify under one general conception of morality.

FMR presupposes some measure of realism. For example, if there are no such things as concepts, beliefs or modes of reasoning, then groups cannot differ with respect at more standards that regulate right and wrong conduct.

Thus, this may involve articulating the good habit that we should acquire, the duties that we should follow in consequences of our behavior on others.

Ethical Theory

COGNITIVISM AND NON-COGNITIVISM

The first and most profound division in ethical theory is between the claim that it is possible to know moral right from wrong and denial of that claim. Because this is claim and encounter-claim about what we can and cannot know, the position which declares we can know is called 'cognitivism' and the contrary position 'non-cognitivism.'

According to cognitivism, there are objective moral truths which can be known, just as we can know other truths about the world. Statements of moral belief, on this view can be true or false just as our statement that something is a certain colour can be true or false. According to the non-cognitivist, by contrast, 'objective' assessment of moral belief is not possible. It is all 'subjective'.

There is no truth or falsity to be discovered. There is only belief, attitude, emotional reaction, and the like. As Hamlet puts it, 'There is nothing either good or bad but thinking makes it so'. When non-cognitivism claims that there are only attitudes, its proponents do not usually mean that moral judgments are simply expressions of one's feelings. Advocates of non-cognitivism acknowledge the essentially social nature of morality by invariably arguing that these are group attitudes.

Consequentialism versus Non-Consequentialism

The greatest divide in cognitivist thinking is between theories which assess moral right and wrong in terms of the consequences of actions and those which do not. Those which do are 'consequentialist' theories; those which do not are 'non-consequentialist'. With consequentialist theories, we look to the results of actions to determine the truth or falsity of moral judgments about them. If what follows from an action is, on balance, of benefit then it is, a good action and so we are right to do it. Conversely, if the outcome is, on balance harmful then the action is 'bad' and we are 'wrong' to do it. For consequentialism, the test of whether an action is right or wrong is whether it is good or bad in the sense of resulting in benefit or harm.

In this case right or wrong is a question of good or bad; and good or bad a question of benefit or harm. For non-consequentialism, there is no immediate appeal to beneficial or harmful consequences to determine good or bad. Divine Command theory offers an illustration of the difference between consequentialism and non-consequentialism. If religious believers were to obey God's commands in order to attain a desirable state after death, or because they believed that obedience was rewarded by material success, then such moves presuppose a consequentialist view of ethic.

If, however, the believer obeys God's commands, not for any expected reward, but for the sole reason that God has commanded them, then he or she presupposes a strictly non-consequentialist account of morality. It is not what follows from our actions which then make them right or wrong but only the fact of their conformity or non-conformity to God's commands.

It is solely in virtue of being activities of such a conforming or non-conforming kind that actions are right or wrong and therefore good or bad. Taken item by item, a consequentialist and non-consequentialist listing of rights and wrongs will probably not differ very much. Of course, there will be some disagreement on substantive moral issues and they are, unsurprisingly, likely to concern just those issues that divide society the most.

Utilitariasm: An ethical of welfare

The best-known consequentialist theory of ethics is called 'utilitarianism'. The name derives from the use of the word utility to denote the capacity in actions to have good results. This choice of word proclaims the consequentialist nature of the theory. Utility means usefulness – under lying the point that it is the usefulness of actions which determines their moral character than anything in the nature of the action itself.

Actions are not good or bad in themselves, but only in what they are good or bad for. Although, strictly speaking, good and bad are the results, while utility and disutility are the capacities for those results, they amount to the same thing in practice and can, for convenience, be treated as synonymous.

CHAPTER 17

Managing Stakeholders

What Stakeholder Management is all about?

Stakeholder management deals with managing all those that have an interest in our business. I call them parents to the organization. These parents include but not limited to employees or staff, management, shareholders, customers, suppliers, lenders of finance and competitors. Managing the aforementioned stakeholders will lead to the success of the business. For the sake of you the reader of this book I have presented part of these stakeholders for you to appreciate the impact they have on the business. Let us now look at the stakeholders one by one.

Manage a Customer

As already pointed out a customer is one of the stakeholders. Failure to mange customers could lead to low sales or no sales. This can give risk to the futurity of the business. To this end it is important that an entrepreneur should seek to meet the expectations of his or her customers, should seek to delight the expectations of his or her customers and more importantly the entrepreneur must amaze his or her customers. As a reminder based on the strategic analysis presented in chapter 13 in pursuit of managing a customer the first logical step is to analyze customers. Customer analysis starts with segmentation. This looks at asking the following questions:

- Who are the biggest customers?
- The most profitable customers
- The most attractive potential customers
- Do the customers fall into any logical groups on the base of needs, motivations or characteristics?

- How should the market be segmented into groups that would require a unique business strategy?

The second strategy in managing a customer revolves around understanding customer behavior. This looks at questions such as:

- Why do customers select and use their favorite brands?
- What elements of the product/service do they value most?
- What are the customers' objectives?
- What are they really buying?
- What changes are occurring in customer motivation?
- What motivates them to go to supplier x or y?
- Customer analysis is trying to be close as possible to them to know what motivates them to go to supplier x

As an entrepreneur you need to convince them that they have been going to wrong products but they should have come to you. It is up to you to convince them that our product, price, place (channels of distribution) and promotional methods will be able to bring solutions to their problems. The idea is feedback and making sure that they always comeback (Customer Relationship Marketing). Always be ahead of customers with new ideas (4Ps).

Manage a Supplier

The art of managing a supplier is vital to the success of an enterprise. For instance, suppliers provide raw materials, goods or services required by an organization in order to function. Suppliers can therefore help or hurt, build or break an organization depending on their ability to provide needed materials at the right time. On its part the supply of labour has a lot of bearing on the success of an organization. Availability of quality and skilled labour tends to determine the past, present and future shape of a firm.

Markets exist because of the interaction of two forces, supply and demand. We then bring the two together in order to get complete picture and understanding of the markets. This is the basis upon economists explain price determination. In our case we are interested in how and why markets work and the interaction of customers and potential suppliers.

Suppliers can affect an industry through their ability to raise prices or reduce the quality of purchased goods and services. A supplier or a group of suppliers is powerful if some of the following factors apply: The supplier industry is dominated by a few companies, but it sells to many, e.g. the petroleum industry. Its commodity is unique and/or it has build up switching costs.

Substitutes are not readily available. Suppliers are able to integrate forward and compete directly with their present customers. Customers buy a small proportion of the supplier's product. The above factors are what are known as micro-factors of environmental influences. On the other hand we have what we call the macro-factors. These macro-factors (also called the social environment) are variables within a corporation's social environment.

They are the general forces that do not directly touch on the short-run activities of the organization but that can, and often do, influence its long-run decisions. These include the following: economic forces that regulate the exchange of materials; money; energy; and information; technological forces that generate problem solving inventions; political-legal forces that allocate power and provide constraining and protecting laws and regulations; sociocultural forces that regulate the values, mores and customs of society.

Managing Competitors

Considering competition is another important aspect organizations need to consider seriously. The competitive environment includes such factors as how the firm rates in the market share, technological innovation, financial strength, involvement in growth industries and the development of its human resources. A firm might be financially sound, have good personnel and dominate its industry, yet if the company is positioned in a declining industry, management may have to take aggressive action to move it to new expanding markets.

One important point to note is that competitive environment is not static, instead it is dynamic and sometimes it could be complex and in some instances it could be volatile. In most industries, corporations are mutually dependent. A competitive move by one firm can be expected to have a noticeable effect on its competitors and thus may cause retaliation or counter-efforts.

Intense rivalry is related to the presence of several factors, including: Number of competitors. When competitors are few and roughly equal in size, they watch each other carefully to make sure that any move by another firm is matched by an equal countermove. Rate of industry growth. For example, any showing in passenger traffic tends to set off price wars in the airline industry because the only path to grow is to take sales away from a competitor.

Amount of fixed costs is another area. For example, because airlines must fly their planes on a schedule regardless of the number of paying passengers for any one flight, they offer cheap standby fares whenever a plane has empty seats. If the only way a manufacturer can increase capacity is in a large increment by building a new plant, it will run that new plant at full capacity to keep its unit costs as low as possible – thus producing so much that the selling price falls throughout the industry.

Rivals that have very different ideas of how to compete are likely to cross paths often and unknowingly challenge each other's position. Sometimes they could be what we call threat of substitutes. Substitute products are those products that appear to be different but can satisfy the same needs as another product. For instance, in Malawi, coffee is a substitute for tea. Substitutes limit the potential returns of an industry by placing a ceiling on the prices firms in the industry can profitably charge.

If the price of coffee goes up high enough, coffee drinkers will slowly begin switching to tea. The price goes up high enough, coffee drinkers will slowly begin switching to tea. The price of tea thus puts a price ceiling on the price of coffee.

New entrants to an industry typically bring to its new capacity, a desire to gain market share, and substantial resources. They are, therefore, threats to an established cooperation. The threat of entry depends on the presence of entry barriers and the reaction that can be expected from existing competitors. An entry barrier is an obstruction that makes it difficult for a company to enter an industry.

Some of the possible barriers to entry are: economies of scale. Economies of scale occur when a firm grows in size and experience reduction in costs as a result of increasing production. Product differentiation. These are the differences in the production or appearances of a product. Sometimes it can occur through high levels of advertising and promotion. Capital requirements. This occurs when an existing firm has huge financial resources to create a significant barrier to entry to any competitor.

Managing Lenders of Finance

Lenders of finance are suppliers of finance or money. This is part of financial management. Financial management is that branch of management accounting which deals with the management of finances in order to achieve the financial objectives of an organization. It deals with the acquisition and allocation of resources among firms, the firm's present and potential activities and projects" Acquisition is concerned with the "financial decision", the generation of funds internally or externally at lowest possible cost. Allocation is concerned with the "investment decision", the use of these funds to achieve corporate financial objectives.

The conventional assumption is that most trading organizations' objective is the maximization of the value of the company for its owners. Since the owners of a company are its shareholders or an entrepreneur, the primary objective of a trading company is said to be "the maximization of shareholders' or an entrepreneurs wealth.

It must be emphasized though that while businesses do have to consider other stakeholders, from a corporate finance perspective, such objectives should only consider other stakeholders, from a corporate finance perspective, such objectives should only be pursued in support of the overriding long-term objective of maximizing shareholders' wealth. Modern finance theory usually assumes that the objective of the firm is to maximize the wealth of shareholders or entrepreneur.

Other possible objectives of the business include: Maximizing Profits Market Share, Obtaining Greater "Managerial Power", Increasing Employee Welfare, Increasing Social Responsibility, and Corporate

Growth. These objectives are operative but tend to be less important than maximizing shareholders' or entrepreneur's wealth.

Lenders of Finance are also called financial institutions. These are financial intermediaries that accept deposits from savers and invest in capital markets. Their functions range from accepting deposits, payment mechanism, borrowing and lending and pooling risks. Classes of these intermediaries include: deposit institutions .e.g. banks, insurance companies, trust companies .e.g. money managers, credit union and Mutual Funds. The financial systems within the financial institutions include: People (Investors and Borrowers), Place (Markets), Product (Securities .e.g. Treasury Bills), Price (Cost of Capital and Cost of Borrowing or simply interest.

Cost of Funds

When you get a loan from a bank, the bank charges interest on the loan. The interest that you get is the cost of lending the money. In other words, the bank could put the money to other use and earn a profit equivalent to or more than the interest that you pay on the loan. Cost of funds or the minimum required return a company should make on its own investments, to earn the cash flows out of which investors can be paid their

Cost of funds has three elements. First, the risk free-rate – this is the return one would get if a security was completely free of any risk. Second, risk free yields are typically on government securities, for example yields on Treasury Bills and third, the premium for business risk – this is an increase in the required rate of return due to compensate for existence of uncertainty about the future of a business.

Cost of funds can be cost of equity or cost of debt. Cost of equity could be estimated by dividend valuation model, which is based on the fundamental analysis theory. This theory states that the market value of shares is directly related to expected future dividends on the shares. The cost of debt capital already issued is the rate of interest (the internal rate of return), which equates the current market price with the discounted future cash receipts from the security.

Weighted Average Cost of Capital

In most cases, a company's funds may be viewed as a pool of resource, that is, a combination of different funds with different costs. Under such circumstances it might seem appropriate to use an average cost of capital for investment approval. High level of debt creates financial risk. Financial risk is measured by gearing ratio.

$$\frac{D}{E + D} = \frac{Debt}{Equity + Debt}$$

Higher gearing will increase KE (cost of equity). Where D stands for Debt and E stands for equity. As the level of gearing increase the cost of debt remain unchanged up to the certain level of gearing. The Ke (cost of equity) rises as the level of gearing increases (need for higher returns). The WACC does not remain constant but rather falls initially as proportional of debt increases and then begins to increase as the rising cost of equi ty/ debt becomes more significant. The optimum level of gearing is where the company's weighted cost of capital is minimized. This assumes that WACC is unchanged coz of the following two factors: Cost of debt remains unchanged on the level of gearing increases. Cost of equity rises in such a way as to keep the WACC constant.

PART FOUR

THE ENVIRONMENT OF BUSINESS

CHAPTER 18

The Business Environment

The business environment consists of the surrounding factors that either help or hinder the development of businesses. There are elements in the business environment.

1. The economic and legal environment
2. The technological environment
3. The competitive environment
4. The social environment
5. The global business environment

Businesses grow and prosper in a health environment. The results are job growth and wealth that makes it possible to have both a high standard of living and a high quality of life. The wrong environmental conditions, in contrast, lead to business failure, loss of jobs and standard of living and quality of life, In short creating the right business environment is the foundation for social progress of all kinds, including good schools, clean air and water, good health care and low rates of crime.

The Economic and Legal Environment

People are willing to start new businesses if they believe that the risk of losing their money isn't too great. Part of the risk involves the economic system and how government works with or against businesses. Government can do a lot to lessen the risk of starting businesses and thus increase entrepreneurship and wealth. For example, a government can keep taxes and regulations to a minimum.

Entrepreneurs are looking for high return on investment (ROI), including the investment of their time. If the government takes away much of what a business earns through high taxes, the ROI may no longer be worth the risk. This is true even within wealthy countries like United States. Countries that have high taxes and restrictive regulations tend to drive entrepreneurs out while countries with low taxes and less restrictive regulations attract entrepreneurs. Laws that encourage entrepreneurship have been enacted all across the world. Some of the tax laws that help businesses include the provisions for deducting home office expenses, business travel and meals and other business expenses.

One way for government to actively promote entrepreneurship is to allow private ownership of businesses. In some countries the government owns most businesses and thus there is little incentive for people to work hard or create profit. All around the world today, however, various countries in which the government formerly owned most businesses are selling those businesses to private individuals to create wealth through privatization process. Privatization is the transfer or sell of government assets to the private sector or individuals.

The Technological Environment

Since prehistoric times, humans have felt the need to create tools that make their jobs easier. Various tools and machines developed throughout history have changed the business environment tremendously, but few technology changes have had a more comprehensive and lasting impact on businesses than the emergency of information technology (IT): Computers, Modems, Cellular Phones and so on. Chief among these is the internet. Although many internet firms have failed in recent years, the Internet will prove to be a major force in business in the coming years.

How technology benefits workers and you. One of the advantages of working for others is that the company often provides the tools and technology to make your job more productive. Technology means everything from phones and copiers to computers, medical imaging devices, personal digital assistants and various software programmes that make business processes more efficient resources. Productivity is the amount of output you generate given the amount of input. The ratio of productivity (Output/Input) must be greater than 1.

The Competitive Environment

The competition among businesses has never been greater than it is today. Some companies have found a competitive edge by focusing on quality. The goals for many companies is zero defects – no mistakes in making the product. However, simply making a high quality product isn't enough to allow a company to stay competitive in world markets. Companies now have to offer both high-quality products and outstanding service at competitive prices (value) with speed advantage.

Manufacturers and service organizations throughout the world have learned that today's customers are very demanding. Not only do they want good quality at low prices, but they want great service as well. In fact, some products in the 21st century will be designed to facilitate, bewitch and delight customers, exceeding and even amazing their customers. Business is becoming customer-driven not management driven as in the past.

This means that customers' wants and needs must come first. Successful organizations must now listen more closely to customers to determine their wants and needs, and then adjust the firm's products, policies, and practices to meet those demands.

Social Environment

The **social environment** consists of the sum total of a society's beliefs, customs, practices and behaviors. It is, to a large extent, an artificial construct that can be contrasted with the natural environment in which we live.

Every society constructs its own social environment. Some of the customs, beliefs, practices and behaviors are similar across cultures, and some are not. For example, an American traveling to Britain will find many familiar practices but not so much if traveling to China.

This social environment created by a society-at-large in which a business functions can be referred to as its **external social environment**. If a business operates in a multicultural society, then the social external social environment is even more complicated because the environment will consist of diverse sub-populations with their own unique values, beliefs, and customs.

A business also has its own social environment. We can refer to this as its **internal social environment**, which is simply the customs, beliefs, practices, and behaviors within the confines of the business. A business has much more control over its internal social environment than it does with its external social environment.

Effects of External Social Environment

A business must utilize and adapt to its external social environment, or it will not survive. A business must be keenly aware of the society's social preferences regarding its needs and wants. These preferences and needs and wants will be influenced by a population's values, beliefs, and practices.

Let's look at some examples. A change in beliefs and values towards energy conservation and global climate change may create a change in consumer preference away from gas guzzling SUVs to hybrid sedans. Some cultures treat the meal as a long social event, and fast food just won't cut it. Social preferences relating to fashion are constantly changing. Skirt lengths go up and down depending upon the years, as do the preference for single-breasted and double-breasted suits.

If a business refuses to adapt to changing social preferences, its sales will drop, and it will fail. Of course, sometimes the change in social preferences may be so large that a business simply can't adapt. For example, a social movement led to the outlawing of alcohol in the early 20th century, which was known as Prohibition. During Prohibition, it was illegal to sell alcohol. Distilleries were put out of business until Prohibition was repealed.

While there are risks with social change, there are also opportunities. Businesses often try to influence social values through the use of marketing, advertising and targeted public relations strategies. Marketing campaigns are used in an attempt to create trends. The fashion industry is a prime example. Public relation campaigns are often used to build up or repair a business' image. For example, BP launched a massive public relations campaign to improve its image after a massive oil leak in the Gulf of Mexico caused by offshore drilling.

Fast food restaurants may include healthier choices on their menus and sponsor health-related activities.

Broader social values will also affect the success of a business. A society that values higher education will provide a better workforce that will lead to more productivity and innovation. Likewise, a society that supports investment in public infrastructure will have access to good transportation and communication systems. And if the social values of a community include a hard work ethic, a business will have access to productive workers and a population that has money to spend on goods and services.

Internal Social Environment

A business also creates a social environment consisting of its own organizational values, norms, customs and practices. Many of these values, norms, and beliefs will mirror the external social environment, but some will be unique to the organization.

Businesses need to operate as a cohesive unit, so it's important that they build a strong and productive organizational culture. It's also important to ensure that the culture is stable and positive. Thus, a business should carefully monitor the relations between its members to detect any hostility or other dysfunction that needs to be corrected.

The Global Environment

The global environment of business is so important that we show it as surrounding all other environmental influences. Two important environmental changes in recent years have been the growth of international competition and the increase of free trade among nations. Japanese manufacturers like Honda, Mitsubish and Sony won much of the market for automobiles and other products by offering good consumers products of higher quality than those made by U.S. manufacturers.

This competition hurt many U.S. industries and many jobs were lost. Recently, U.S. businesses have become more competitive and Japan's economy is now suffering. Today, manufacturers in countries such as China, India, South Korea and Mexico can produce high – quality goods at low prices because their workers are paid less money than U.S. workers and because they have learned quality concepts from Japanese, German and U.S. producers.

CHAPTER 19

Managing Risk with Profit

As indicated in earlier chapters one of the ways to become a success is to start a business. A business is any activity that seeks to provide goods and services to others while operating at a profit. Profit is the amount of money a business earns above and beyond what it spends. In simple terms profit can be defined as revenue above costs. Since not all businesses make a profit starting a business can be a risky proposition.

As said earlier an entrepreneur is a person who risks time and money to start and manage a business. Once an entrepreneur has started a business there is usually a need for good managers and other workers to keep the business going. However, not all entrepreneurs are skilled at being managers. Business provides people with opportunity to become wealthy.

Profit remember is the amount of money a business earns above and beyond what it pays out for salaries and other expenses. Revenue is the total amount of money a business takes during a given period by selling goods and services. A loss occurs when a business's expenses are more than its revenue. If a business loses money over time it will likely have to close ans this will put its employees out of work. Therefore starting business involves risk. Risk is a chance an entrepreneur takes of losing time and money on a business that may not prove profitable. Even companies that do make profit not all companies make the same amount. Those companies that take high risk make the most profit. There is a saying that says, "the higher the risk the higher the returns." As a business owner you need to do research to find the right balance between risk and profit for you.

Business Add to the Standard of Living and Quality of Life

Entrepreneurs such as Bill Gates (Microsoft) not only become wealthy themselves by starting successful businesses; they also provide employment for other people. Employees pay taxes which government uses to finance the public sector. Businesses too, pay taxes to government and that money can be used to schools, hospitals and other such facilities. Thus the wealth businesses generate and taxes they pay help every one in their communities. A nation's businesses are part of an economic system that contributes to the standard of living and quality of life for everyone in the country.

The term **standard of living**refers to the amount of goods and services people can buy with their money. However, the cost of goods differ from country to country. The reasons why goods cost more in one country versus the other include high taxes and stricter government regulations. Funding the right level of taxes and regulation is an important step towards making a country prosperous.

The term **quality of life** refers to the general well-being of society in terms of political freedom, a clean natural environment, education, health care, safety, free time and everything else that leads to satisfaction and joy. Maintaining a high quality of life requires the combined efforts of businesses, non - profit organizations and government agencies. The more money businesses create, the more is potentially available to improve the quality of life for everyone.

Entrepreneurship versus Working for Others

There are two ways to succeed in business. One way is to rise up through the ranks of large corporations. The advantage of working for others is that someone else assumes the entrepreneurial risk and provides you with benefits such as paid vacation time and health insurance. Most people choose that option. It is a very good option and can lead to a happy prosperous life. Businesses need good managers to succeed and all workers contribute to producing and marketing the goods and services that increase the quality of life and standard of living for others.

The other more risk part is to start your own business. Thus, it takes a brave person to start a business. Further, more as an entrepreneur you do not receive any benefits such as paid vacation and health insurance. You have to provide them for yourself.

CHAPTER 20

Managing the Business in a Dynamic and Complex Environment

A **dynamic environment** is changing rapidly. Managers must react quickly and organizations must be flexible to respond. Today's **business environment** is generally very **dynamic**. Technology, consumer tastes, laws and regulations, political leaders, and international conditions are all changing rapidly and dramatically.

It has been pointed out that an organization's environment contains many influences on that organization. It is therefore always tempting to begin an analysis of that environment by reviewing its parts in an attempt to decide how they exert an influence. Strategic decisions are by their very nature made in situations of uncertainty. Thus environmental uncertainty increases the more environmental conditions are dynamic or the more they are complex.

Understanding Simple/Static Conditions

In simple/ static conditions an organization is faced with an environment which is not too difficult to understand and is not going significant change. Usually the organization is in a monopoly kind of market structure. Thus their processes are relatively straight forward, their competition and markets are likely to be fixed over time.

Understanding Dynamic and Complex Conditions

In dynamic conditions the environment is changing. To cope up with uncertainty there should be organizational responses and information gathering. The lesson, in straightforward terms is that in dynamic conditions it makes more sense.

Economic Dynamics

Economic changes can spark a dynamic environment geography too. For example, in an online article Business Case Studies reports the impact of falling interest rates on a business, and specifically how falling rates may allow a business or its competitors to expand, rapidly changing the industry's growth rate. Falling prices for needed raw resources may do the same. Look for circumstances that provide an impetus for action.

Societal Dynamics

By the theory of environmental dynamics, sociocultural conditions can also act to catalyze the business environment. Social networking has changed industry thinking about how to connect with markets. In the news industry, for instance, anchors now regularly ask viewers to tweet information or to follow them on Facebook, seeking to interact rather than merely present.

Shifting demographics may also lead to a dynamic environment, as businesses respond with new and improved products and services.

Technological Dynamics

A new invention or discovery can revolutionize an industry. The small business owner should be on the lookout for innovations that promise to change the way business is conducted. The invention of the printing press, the automobile and refrigeration opened opportunities for those who could see the implications of the new technologies.

Sometimes a breakthrough heralds a period of continual technological advancement. Such is the case in the cellphone industry. Releasing phones from wall jacks was revolutionary enough. Now phones can open garage doors. Such continuous change signals a dynamic business environment.

Market Dynamics

New players in a marketplace can become change agents, especially if these competitors are aggressive or employ new approaches to courting customers or creating products. Additionally, the markets themselves may create dynamic conditions. For instance, untapped markets in foreign locations may open, presenting vast new opportunities. Examining market events, the small business owner should consider both direct and indirect effects on the company. What affects a company's suppliers, for instance, may affect the small business itself.

For purposes of strategic planning, an environment is dynamic in nature if it is affected by a variety of factors, such as technological, socio-economic, governmental, legal, and competitive and supply chain events.

The more readily that any of these factors change, the more dynamic the company's operating environment. The more volatile and complex an operating environment, the larger the number of changes, the greater the significance of those changes and the more frequently the changes occur.

The larger the number of changes, the greater their significance, and the more frequent the changes, the greater the risk that change has a significant positive or negative impact on a company's strategic management functions and its operations. Any adverse effects are compounded by management's failure to understand the changes and their effects.

When rapid or sudden change occurs, such as technological innovation or political upheaval, the environmental dynamism that results may negate a company's long-held competitive advantage. Most certainly, the turbulence affects market conditions that underscore a company's strategic plan and makes strategic management processes more difficult.

Strategic Management in Dynamic Environments

Strategy is a plan of action that's designed to achieve a goal. During the typically systematic and detailed planning process, participants make decisions related to actions employees will take, such as using certain financial or physical resources to achieve agreed-upon strategic goals.

If a company is to remain viable in a dynamic environment, it must respond quickly to rapid changes with new or revised strategic options. The more adaptive and flexible a company, the better its performance will be in unpredictable times. This adaptability requires that management encourage personnel to develop flexible competencies and the capabilities they need to understand and respond to environmental changes in an appropriate manner.

Evolution of Strategic Plans

A dynamic environment can significantly curtail a company's efforts to accomplish established goals, such as increasing market share or establishing a beachhead in another country. What's worse, some strategic planning tools are ineffective in turbulent times.

For these reasons, the perception of strategy is changing from that of structured, detailed plans to guidelines that might be considered in certain situations. This change in concept, however, doesn't negate the usefulness of thinking through the actions a company might take given a certain set of circumstances.

PART FIVE

MANAGING TIMES OF BUSINESS DOWNTURN

CHAPTER 21

Managing Performance in a Down Turn

The reality to the down turns is recurring fact of life in every industry. While acknowledging that the normal practice of cost cutting and downsizing in these conditions is not unreasonable. However, contrary to the normal practice there is an opportunity in any crisis. While aggressive cost management is extremely important during this period, it is also equally important during an upturn. Lay offs for example, are often implemented as away of holding down costs, but do they really make financial sense when compared to purchasing costs?

Despite frequent findings that purchasing costs far exceed labour costs for most businesses. It is labour costs that often seem to be the focus of most cost – reduction strategies. Put simply, a business shouldn't act one way in good times and another in bad times.

The ensuring views on downsizing in a downturn appear to point out that while downsizing and disciplined cost management are sensible initiatives to improving business performance and profitability, these measures are not a sole means to achieveing superior business performance in themselves.

A critical focus on the growth objective

Not all growth is good. Growth at all costs or for its own sake can be a recipe for disaster. Focusing on growth does not mean that operational efficiency must be ignored but that it is not the dominant performance driver. Both growth and efficiency are required for business success.

The pursuit of size of a firm has proven even less robust a strategy than profitability. This is a call to carefully examine the strategies that are available to select one that is best suited for the market environment in question. On the downside of a bad growth it is simply more fun and stimulating to create growth than to improve productivity by downsizing. There are three assertions to this.

Firstly, is that if a business isn't growing sustainably and profitably it is dying. Secondly, that any business can grow profitably and that there is no such a thing as a mature business. The thirs assertion is that sustainable growth is profitable and capital efficient. These views on growth present two important points.

The first is that growth aught to be treated as an imperative for all business organizations. Without growth, businesses may stagnate decline and eventuary face natural death. The second point being propagated in these views is a line of caution to entrepreneurs that while the drive for growth might sound pleasing.

It might be the dosage for further damage to business profitability if taken out of mere obsession for it. Growth must be sustainable. A business must therefore carefully examine how it aught to embrace the growth initiative.

A strategic alternative for declining markets

The discussions of strategies for shrinking industries usually focus on creativity, innovation, divestment and harvest strategies. There are certain advantages and disadvantages to each market. Receiving an inheritance can also be helpful but many do not have this opportion and even those who do often do not know how to properly manage and grow this money once they have it.

CHAPTER 22

Creativity, Innovation and Invention

After alII read on the blogs and Twitter, and all the new innovation programmes and initiatives in state and local governments. I feel the need to revisit the definitions of these key words: innovation, creativity and inventions.

First the innovation definitions

As indicated earlier an Entrepreneur is a person who starts a new business. That is not necessarily innovative, but it can create new jobs and new wealth, so it is valuable. Sometimes Entrepreneurs create new wealth, so it is valuable. Sometimes, Entrepreneurs create businesses based on new ideas, either through inventions or new inventions. However, a person running a McDonald's is also an Entrepreneur, but not necessarily innovative.

What is Creativity?

Creativity simply means creating value and it is directly linked with invention and it is turned into practical reality through innovation. Entrepreneurship then sets that innovation in the context of an enterprise which is something of recognized value.

Creativity is the act of turning new and imaginative ideas into reality. Creativity is characterized by the ability to perceive the world in new ways, to find hidden patterns, to make connections between seemingly unrelated phenomena, and to generate solutions. *Creativity involves two processes: thinking, then producing. If you have ideas, but donot act on them, you are imaginative but not creative.*

"Creativity is the process of bringing something new into being. Creativity requires passion and commitment. It brings to our awareness what was previously hidden and points to new life. The experience is one of heightened consciousness: ecstasy." – Rollo May, The Courage to Create *is* this possible in business? I believe so, but you have to be willing to take risks and progress through discomfort to get to the finish line.

> "A product is creative when it is (a) novel and (b) appropriate. A novel product is original not predictable. The bigger the concept, and the more the product stimulates further work and ideas, themore the product is creative."
>
> —Sternberg &Lubart, *Defying the Crowd*

What is Innovation?

Innovation is the implementation of a new or significantly improved product, service or process that creates value for business, government or society. Some people say creativity has nothing to do with innovation— that innovation is a discipline, implying that creativity is not. Well, I disagree. Creativity is also a discipline, and a crucial part of the innovation equation. There *is* no innovation without creativity. The key metric in both creativity and innovation is value creation.

An inventor is someone who creates a new to the world product or solution. Inventions become interesting when they create value for the inventor or consumers or the world at large. Inventors are innovative, but innovative solutions donot have to be inventions. Many innovations are new business models, new services experience that are not necessarily "innovations."

Just as Entrepreneurs are not defined simply as owner – managers, entrepreneurial firms are not defined, necessarily, in terms of size. But there are linkages between size and innovation. Few small firms introduce really new products into their product mix. Even fewer introduce really new products into the economy as a whole. This role is likely to be taken by larger firms because of the resources they command. However, small firms can and often do introduce products or services that are clearly differentiated from those of the competition. Indeed, this ability to differentiate clearly is a major element in the success. Is this innovation?

Perhaps it is, but one would have to stretch Schumpeter's first or even his third criterion (opening new market to accommodate it).

Innovation is the process of translating an idea or invention into a good or service that createsvalue or for which customers will pay. To be called an innovation, an idea must be replicable at an economicalcost and must satisfy a specific need. Innovation involves deliberate application of information, imagination and initiative in deriving greater or different values from resources, and includes all processes by which new ideas are generated and converted into useful products.

In business, innovation often results when ideas are applied by the company in order to further satisfy the needs and expectations of the customers. In a social context, innovation helps create new methods for alliance creation, joint venturing, flexible work hours, and creation of buyers' purchasing power.

Innovations are divided into two broad categories:

1. *Evolutionary innovations* (continuous or dynamic evolutionary innovation) that are brought about by many incremental advances in technology or processes and
2. *Revolutionary innovations* (also called discontinuous innovations) which are often disruptive and new.

Innovation is synonymous with risk-taking and organizations that create revolutionary products or technologies take on the greatest risk because they create new markets. Imitators take less risk because they will start with an innovator's product and take a more effective approach. Examples are IBM with its PC against AppleComputer, Compaq with its cheaper PC's against IBM, and Dell with its still-cheaper clones against Compaq.

Use innovation in a sentence

By allowing the developer of an innovation to reap the rewards of his efforts, we create an environment that encourages innovative thinking and hard work. Sofia was much happier at this workplace: they celebrated innovation and rewarded employees who came up with new ideas and better ways of doing things. Some people praise technology and innovation but I think we should go back to the dark ages because as a society we would be much happier.

Therefore, an innovation can also be defined as a new idea that is put into a valuable or profitable action. An innovation can be created by an inventor who then licenses his or her invention to others to commercialize the concept in his or her capacity as an Entrepreneur. An innovation can be created by the organization to disrupt an existing market. Innovation can happen in organization of any size. Additionally, there is innovation in governments, in academic institutions and in not – for profits. We typically donot think of these organizations as entrepreneurial or as inventing new things yet they can be innovative. Further, innovations can be new products, but can also be new service models, new business models and new customer experiences.

The ability to sport opportunities and to innovate are the most important distinguished features of Entrepreneurs. Innovation is the prime tool Entrepreneurs use to create or exploit opportunity. These characteristics set Entrepreneurs apart from owner – managers. Entrepreneurs link innovation to the market place so as to exploit an opportunity and make their business grow.

We need all the three of these concepts work well to succeed. We need inventors to create new products and new processes and we need Entrepreneurs to disrupt existing markets and bring these new products and services to the market. We also need innovation from large existing firms, because without innovation they stagnate and die. When we talk about innovation, invention and Entrepreneurs and when we put policies in place to encourage certain types of activities or investments we need to understand the implications and ramifications of those words and actions. While closely related, invention, innovation and Entrepreneurs are not the same things and should not be treated in the same fashion.

There is a fundamental difference between an innovator and an inventor, writes digital Entrepreneur Tom Grasty in a great column over at MediaShift Idea Lab.

Invention is the "creation of a product or introduction of a process for the first time." Thomas Edison was an inventor.

Innovation **happens when someone "improves on or makes a significant contribution" to something that has already been invented.**

Okay, so they are different. What does that mean for Entrepreneurs?

You cannot just focus on innovation and you cannot just focus on invention. That is not what an Entrepreneur does. The Entrepreneur recognizes the potential early on, then turns it into something big.

Grasty explains it with an analogy: "If invention is a pebble tossed in the pond, innovation is the rippling effect that pebble causes. Someone has to toss the pebble. That is the inventor. Someone has to recognize the ripple to eventually become a wave. That is the Entrepreneur.

"Entrepreneurs don not stop at the water's edge. They watch the ripples and spot the next big wave *before* it happens. And it is the act of anticipating and riding that "next big wave" that drives the innovative nature in every entrepreneur."

Chapter 23

Divestment

Divestment is a form of retrenchment strategy used by businesses when they downsize the scope of their business activities. Divestment usually involves eliminating a portion of a business.

Firms may elect to sell, close, or spin-off a strategic business unit, major operating division, or product line. This move often is the final decision to eliminate unrelated, unprofitable, or unmanageable operations.

Divestment is commonly the consequence of a growth strategy. Much of the corporate downsizing has been the result of acquisitions and takeovers. Firms often acquired other businesses with operations in areas with which the acquiring firm had little experience. After trying for a number of years to integrate the new activities into the existing organization, many firms have elected to divest themselves of portions of the business in order to concentrate on those activities in which they had a competitive advantage.

Reasons to Divest

In most cases it is not immediately obvious that a unit should be divested. Many times management will attempt to increase investment as a means of giving the unit an opportunity to turn its performance around. Portfolio models such as the Boston Consulting Group (BCG) Model or General Electric's Business Screen can be used to identify operations in need of divestment. For example, products or business operations identified as "dogs" in the BCG Model are prime candidates for divestment.

Decisions to divest may be made for a number of reasons:

Market Share Too Small

Firms may divest when their market share is too small for them to be competitive or when the market is too small to provide the expected rates of return.

Availability of Better Alternatives

Firms may also decide to divest because they see better investment opportunities. Organizations have limited resources. They are often able to divert resources from a marginally profitable line of business to one where the same resources can be used to achieve a greater rate of return.

Need for Increased Investment

Firms sometimes reach a point where continuing to maintain an operation is going to require large investments in equipment, advertising, research and development, and so forth to remain viable. Rather than invest the monetary and management resources, firms may elect to divest that portion of the business.

Lack of Strategic Fit

A common reason for divesting is that the acquired business is not consistent with the image and strategies of the firm. This can be the result of acquiring a diversified business. It may also result from decisions to restructure and refocus the existing business.

Legal Pressures to Divest

Firms may be forced to divest operations to avoid penalties for restraint of trade.

Implementation of Divestment Strategies:

Firms may pursue a divestment strategy by spinning off a portion of the business and allowing it to operate as an independent business entity.

Firms may also divest by selling a portion of the business to another organization. Another way to implement a divestment decision is to simply close a portion of the firm's operations.

Many divestments are blocked by management's expectations for the operation. Firms may expect demand for the product to pick up. Management may also see the poor performance as a temporary setback that can be overcome with time and patience. Decisions to divest a business may be seen as an admission of failure on the part of management and may lead to escalating commitment to the struggling business as a way of protecting management's ego and public image.

Divestment is not usually the first choice of strategy for a business. However, as product demand changes and firms alter their strategies, there will almost always be some portion of the business that is not performing to management's expectations. Such an operation is a prime target for divestment and may well leave the company in a stronger competitive position if it is divested.

CHAPTER 24

Harvesting

When you have the power to get wealth you will never be at a loss for great business ideas you need to get what you want. The anointing comes with wisdom. Harvesting is most often referring to selling a business or product line, as when a company sells a product line or division or a family sells a business. Harvesting is also occasionally used to refer to sales of a product or product line towards the end of a product life cycle.

Harvesting is therefore a strategy in which investment in a particular line of business is reduced or eliminated because the revenue brought in by additional investment would not warrant the expense. A harvest strategy is employed when a line of business is considered to be a cash cow, meaning that the brand is mature and is unlikely to grow if more investment is added.

The company will instead siphon off the revenue that the cash cow brings in until the brand is no longer profitable. Simply put harvesting is the final phase in the entrepreneurial value creation process, which includes building, growing, and harvesting.

Harvesting is the process entrepreneurs and investors use to exit a business and liquidate their investment in a firm. While all three phases are important pieces of the entrepreneurial process, many entrepreneurs who fail to execute a successful harvest do not realize the full benefits of their years of labor.

Harvesting is the means for capturing or unlocking value, reducing risk, and creating exit options. It is about more than money, as it also involves personal and non-financial considerations. As a consequence, even upon realizing an acceptable monetary value for the firm, an entrepreneur who is not prepared for the lifestyle transition that accompanies the harvest may come away disappointed with the overall outcome. Thus, crafting a harvest strategy is as essential to the entrepreneur's personal success as it is to his or her financial success.

The message to the entrepreneur is this: the time to develop an effective harvest strategy is now, not later. As a firm moves toward the harvest, two questions regarding value are of primary importance. First, are the current owners/managers creating value? You can harvest only what you have created.

CHAPTER 25

Avoid Pitfalls in Entrepreneurship

To ensure deliberate efforts to avoid pitfalls in entrepreneurship there is need to undersyand why businesses fail. Businesses fail for many reasons. The following list includes some of the most common reasons:

1 – Lack of planning

Businesses fail because of the lack of short-term and long-term planning. Your plan should include where your business will be in the next few months to the next few years. Include measurable goals and results. The right plan will include specific to-do lists with dates and deadlines. Failure to plan will damage your business.

2 – Leadership failure

Businesses fail because of poor leadership. The leadership must be able to make the right decisions most of the time. From financial management to employee management, leadership failures will trickle down to every aspect of your business. The most successful entrepreneurs learn, study, and reach out to mentors to improve their leadership skills.

3 – No differentiation

It is not enough to have a great product. You also have to develop a unique value proposition, without you will get lost among the competition. What sets your business apart from the competition? What makes your business unique? It is important that you understand what your competitors do better than you. If fail to differentiate, you will fail to build a brand.

4 – Ignoring customer needs

Every business will tell you that the customer is #1, but only a small percentage acts that way. Businesses that fail lose touch with their customers. Keep an eye on the trending values of your customers. Find out if they still love your products. Do they want new features? What are they saying? Are you listening? I once talked to the CEO of a training company who told me that they don't respond to negative reviews because they are unimportant. What? Are you kidding me?

5 – Inability to learn from failure

We all know that failure is usually bad, yet it is rare that businesses learn from failure. Realistically, businesses that fail, fail for multiple reasons. Often entrepreneurs are oblivious about their mistakes. Learning from failures is difficult.

6 – Poor management

Examples of poor management are an inability to listen, micro-managing – AKA lack of trust, working without standard or systems, poor communication, and lack of feedback.

7 – Lack of capital

It can lead to the inability to attract investors. Lack of capital is an alarming sign. It shows that a business might not be able to pay its bills, loan, and other financial commitments. Lack of capital makes it difficult to grow the business and it may jeopardize day-to-day operations.

8 – Premature scaling

Scaling is a good thing if it is done at the right time. To put it simply, if you scale your business prematurely, you will destroy it. For example, you could be hiring too many people too quickly, or spend too much on marketing. Don't scale your business unless you are ready.

9 – Poor location

Poor location is a disadvantage that might be too much to overcome. If your business relies on foot traffic, location is a strategic necessity. A poor location might make your customer acquisition costs too high.

10 – Lack of profit

Revenue is not the same as profit. As an entrepreneur, you must keep your eyes on profitability at all times. Profit allows for growth. According to Small Business Trends, only 40% of small businesses are profitable, 30% break even, and 30% are losing money.

11 – Inadequate inventory management

Too little inventory will hurt your sales. Too much inventory will hurt your profitability.

12 – Poor financial management

Use a professional accounting software like Freshbooks. Keep records of all financial records and always make decisions based on the information you get from real data. Know where you stand all the time. If numbers are not your thing, hire a financial professional to explain and train you to understand, at least the basics.

13 – Lack of focus

Without focus, your business will lose it the competitive edge. It is impossible to have a broad strategy on a startup budget. What makes startups succeed is their ability to quickly pivot, and the lack of focus leads to the inability to make the necessary adjustments.

14 – Personal use of business funds

Your business is not your personal bank account.

15 – Overexpansion

It is easy to make the mistake of expanding your business into too many verticals. Before you enter new markets make sure you maximize your existing market.

17 – No succession plan

Future leaders should be identified in advance. Without an effective succession plan, your business is unprepared to fill openings in created by retirements, unexpected departures, or death.

18 – Wrong partner

It's no secret that it is easier to succeed in business with the right partners. The wrong business partner will, at the very least hurt, or, at worst, destroy your company.

If you are serious about making it as entrepreneurs, focus on the following:

19 – Make a plan

It all begins with planning. The biggest mistake many entrepreneurs make as they start their ventures is that they don't sit down and write a business plan. The goal is to keep it concise. Don't treat it like a business school project. Leave writing a 50,000-word business plan to academics. Let them waste their time. You can do a great business plan in one or two pages. There are some great books on business plans such as "The Secrets to Writing a Successful Business Plan" and "Successful Business Plan".

CHAPTER 26

✦

Considering Succession Plan

Succession Planning is a process for identifying and developing internal people with the potential to fill key business leadership positions in the company. Succession planning increases the availability of experienced and capable employees that are prepared to assume these roles as they become available. Taken narrowly, "replacement planning" for key roles is the heart of succession planning.

Effective succession or talent-pool management concerns itself with building a series of feeder groups up and down the entire leadership pipeline or progression. In contrast, replacement planning is focused narrowly on identifying specific back-up candidates for given senior management positions. For the most part position-driven replacement planning (often referred to as the "truck scenario") is a forecast, which research indicates does not have substantial impact on outcomes.

Fundamental to the succession-management process is an underlying philosophy that argues that top talent in the corporation must be managed for the greater good of the enterprise. Merck and other companies argue that a "talent mindset" must be part of the leadership culture for these practices to be effective.

Succession planning is a process whereby an organization ensures that employees are recruited and developed to fill each key role within the company. Through your succesion planning process, you recruit superior employees, develop their knowledge, skills, and abilities, and prepare them for advancement or promotion into ever more challenging roles. Actively pursuing succession planning ensures that employees are constantly developed to fill each needed role. As your organization expands, loses key employees, provides promotional opportunities, and increases sales, your succession planning guarantees that you have employees on hand ready and waiting to fill new roles.

According to a 2006 Canadian Federation of Independent Business survey, slightly more than one third of independent business owners plan to exit their business within the next 5 years and within the next 10 years two-thirds of owners plan to exit their business. The survey also found that small and medium sized enterprises are not adequately prepared for their business succession: only 10% of owners have a formal, written succession plan; 38% have an informal, unwritten plan; and the remaining 52% do not have any succession plan at all.

The results are backed by a 2004 CIBC survey which suggests that succession planning is increasingly becoming a critical issue. By 2010, CIBC estimates that $1.2 trillion in business assets are poised to change hands. Research indicates many succession-planning initiatives fall short of their intent (Corporate Leadership Council, 1998). "Bench strength," as it is commonly called, remains a stubborn problem in many if not most companies. Studies indicate that companies that report the greatest gains from succession planning feature high ownership by the CEO and high degrees of engagement among the larger leadership team.

Research indicates that clear objectives are critical to establishing effective succession planning. These objectives tend to be core to many or most companies that have well-established practices: identify those with the potential to assume greater responsibility in the organization; provide critical development experiences to those that can move into key roles; engage the leadership in supporting the development of high-potential leaders; build a data base that can be used to make better staffing decisions for key jobs; In other companies these additional objectives may be embedded in the succession process; improve employee commitment and retention; meet the career development expectations of existing employees and Counter the increasing difficulty and costs of recruiting employees externally.

Succession Planning with Your Board

Succession planning is a means for an organization to ensure its continued effective performance through leadership continuity. For an organization to plan for the replacement of key leaders, potential leaders must first be identified and prepared to take on those roles. It is not enough to select people in the organization who seem "right" for the job. Not only should the experience and duties be considered, but also the personality, the leadership skills, and the readiness for taking on a key leadership role.

Next, determine which members to consider for the leadership positions. It is best to identify this group with an objective system instead of just selecting "favorites." One option is for members to self-select into the process. This way, those who are already interested in the leadership roles will volunteer.

They may be the most likely to take it seriously. Several "hopefuls" should be identified for each position to be filled. This allows the potential leaders to be "groomed," trained, and mentored for the possibility of filling the leadership positions. When the time comes for the position to be filled, there will be several people from which to choose, all of whom have had the time to develop for the new role. At least one of them may be ready to meet the requirements.

In order to prepare potential leaders, the gap between what they are ready for now and what preparation they need to be ready for the job when it is available needs to be determined. This information can help determine what training, experience, and mentoring is needed. By considering their past performance as a volunteer, past experience, fit with the organizational culture, and other members' acceptance of them as a potential leader, the best fit can be determined. Also, ensure that the potential leaders are willing to carry out the organization's mission and to continue the organization's philosophy and culture.

Once the potential leaders have been identified, a plan for each of them should be developed. Each potential leader should be assigned a mentor; this mentor should be the person whom they may replace. The mentor and the potential leader should form a teacher-student relationship. When issues arise that need problem solving or decision making, the leader should meet with the potential leader to ask how he or she would handle the situation.

Allow the potential leaders time to "shadow" the leaders. If possible, allow them to attend board meetings and participate in the decision making. This is a great way to see how they problem solve and interact.

The leaders may even want to present the potential leaders with a problem and allow them to solve it as a group without any benefit of the leaders' input. See if the potential leaders would react in a way that is suitable or favorable.

Also allow them to participate in goal-setting activities, such as strategic planning or budgeting. It is important to see them in action. This process should not be a means for the leaders to choose the person most like them. Because a potential leader solves problems the same way as the leader does not make him or her the best candidate.

The board may want to plan to conduct interviews with each candidate, assessing his or her abilities to make decisions, solve problems, behave appropriately in sensitive situations and lead those who will report to him or her. If appropriate, it is a good idea to allow direct reports to have some say in who will lead them.

Finally, evaluate the succession planning efforts. What went well? What went wrong? What could be done differently? Make suggestions and recommendations for improving the process so that it runs more smoothly next time. If all goes as planned, the succession planning process will ensure a smooth transition and a new leader who is prepared for his or her role in the organization.

Succession Planning Process

The following steps should be followed: determine the key leaders for whom successors will be identified; identify the competencies of current key leaders; Identify experience and duties required; identify personality, political savvy, judgement; identify leadership skills; select the high-potential members who will participate in succession planning; identify gap between what the high-potential members are able to do presently and what they must do in the leadership role; create a development plan for each high-potential member to prepare him or her for the leadership position; perform development activities with each high-potential member; interview and select a member for the new leadership position and evaluate succession planning efforts and make changes to program based on evaluation for future programs.

4 Tips For Efficient Succession Planning

One of the most common leadership development questions that I hear from executives is, "Why does succession planning feel like such a waste of time?" Many of the CEOs we talk with these days express concern about the lack of bench strength in their companies. They are very worried that they lack sufficient "ready now" candidates to replace planned & unplanned losses of key leaders. As a result, the future continuity and performance of the business is at risk.

These same executives also tell us that their companies have been doing succession planning for years. On average, the executives we meet give their succession planning process a grade of C+ and they give their execution of succession plans a grade of D. If you are among the companies who are not happy with the impact of your succession planning process, you have plenty of company. Here are four practical ideas on how you can get more impact from your organization's succession planning efforts.

1. Change the name of the process to from Succession Planning to Succession Development.

Plans do not develop anyone — only development experiences develop people. We see many companies put more effort and attention into the planning process than they do into the development process. Succession planning processes have lots of to-do's — forms, charts, meetings, due dates and checklists. They sometimes create a false sense that the planning process is an end in itself rather than a precursor to real development. Many humans fall into the same trap regarding physical fitness.

We have may have fantastic plans in place to lose weight. We may be very proud of our plans, which include detailed daily goals for diet, alcohol consumption, and exercise. And if our execution were half as impressive as our planning, we would be very svelte. Our focus should be on weight loss, not planning for weight loss.

2. *Measure outcomes, not process*

This change of emphasis is important for several reasons. First, executives pay attention to what gets measured and what gets rewarded. If leadership development is not enough of a priority for the company to establish goals and track progress against those goals, it will be difficult to make any succession planning process work. Second, the act of engaging with senior executives to establish these goals will build support for succession planning and ownership for leadership development. Third, these results will help guide future efforts and mid-course corrections.

The metrics a company could establish for Succession Development might include goals like the percent of executive level vacancies that are actually filled with an internal promotion vs. an external hire, or the percent of promotions that actually come from the high-potential pool. Too often, we find companies measure only the percent of managers that had completed succession plans in place.

3. Keep it simple.

We sometimes find companies adding excessively complex assessment criteria to the succession planning process in an effort to improve the quality of the assessment. Some of these criteria are challenging even for behavioral scientists to assess, much less the average line manager.

Since the planning process is only a precursor to focus the development, it doesn't need to be perfect. More sophisticated assessments can be built into the development process and administered by a competent coach.

4. Stay realistic.

Following are two classic examples how succession plans may lack realism: The head of engineering is a high performing leader who has the potential to be CEO. She has always been in an engineering role. If she had sales experience, she would be even more ready to be the CEO so her development plan is written to include a job move to be head of sales. However, this company would never take the risk of putting someone without sales experience in the top sales job — so her development plan perpetually says, "move to a sales job" even though that will never happen.

The CEO is a high performing leader who has passed all the assessment criteria to be a high potential, ready-now candidate for the CEO job. He is told he is the top candidate. However, the CEO can't stand the guy, and as a result, he will never get the job as long as that CEO has a say in the matter.

While development plans and succession charts aren't promises, they are often communicated as such and can lead to frustration if they aren't realistic. Bottom line, don't jerk around high performing leaders with unrealistic development expectations. Only give the promise of succession if there is a realistic chance of its happening!

We believe the four suggestions above can help shift your organization's focus from planning to development — and achieve increased depth in your bench strength. Please send us your suggestions on succession planning and how the process can be improved. Any of your personal examples are welcome. As companies begin to develop a succession planning process, they should consider these fundamental issues:

High potential vs. Everyone

Some companies focus all of their succession planning efforts on "high potential individuals," whereas others create a succession plan for everyone from the moment they are onboard. The benefit of focusing on high-potential workers is you can channel more resources and coaching toward those employees with the greatest promise. The risk is that you overlook great people and alienate and frustrate the rest of the employees, which can impact morale and turnover. "Most successful organization focus on everyone," says Dan Schneider, cultural architect at advisory firm The Rawls Group.

Hiring from within vs. bringing in someone new

Developing leaders internally takes time and effort, but these home-grown candidates are more likely to be successful than external candidates. According to a 2012 study by Matthew Bidwell, an assistant professor at the University of Pennsylvania's Wharton School, external hires are 61 percent more likely to be laid off or fired, and 21 percent more likely than internal hires to leave a job on their own accord.

These outside hires also get paid more, but get lower marks in performance reviews during their first two years on the job. However, internal hires aren't always an option. Fully 38 percent of firms anticipate they will need to recruit externally for C-level roles in the next 12 months. Internal candidates are also not always the best choice. If a company wants to move in a dramatically different direction, or its current leaders leave before the next generation is ready, companies need to be open to bringing in someone from the outside.

Factoring diversity into decision-making. Managers often seek people who are like them for mentoring and promotion, which often leads to a plethora of white men leading organizations. If companies want diversity in their leadership, the succession planning initiative should include steps that actively promote women and minorities for leadership opportunities, and train managers on how to encourage diversity on their teams.

Making sure you have support from the top. HR can build a great talent development plan, but without active support from leadership, it won't have the desired impact. HR leaders can't force executives to support their efforts but they can align talent management efforts with strategic plans and educate executives and managers about the business value of succession planning efforts.

Fluor's leaders develop their own replacements

At Fluor Corp., the global construction and engineering firm headquartered in Irving, Texas, talent management efforts are directly aligned with long-term strategic goals, and executives are viewed as the company's corporate talent scouts.

"Having a robust succession planning and talent review program and culture is just good business," says Glen Gilkey, Fluor's senior vice president of HR. "It helps mitigate the risk that leadership will be a constraint to growth."

Part of every executive's job is to identify high-performing employees and help them build their skills and experiences so they can move up the corporate ranks, Gilkey says. "Leaders are held accountable for the development of their people even if it means moving them to another division," he says.

Flour relies on a 70-20-10 model of talent development with 70 percent of the development coming from experience, 20 percent from coaching and 10 percent from classroom or other training. Leaders are expected to look for opportunities for employees to gain experience and to provide them with the necessary support and coaching to be successful, Gilkey says.

Conclusion

These may be economic hard times for the majority but for the entrepreneurs, these are times teeming with economic potential. Not only is now the time to have your own business, but there has never been a better time than right now. This is a call to start your own business today. I believe that after reading this book you have learned many things about how you can start your own business that will help you achieve your goals in life. The next step is to learn how to apply all the information that you have learned from this book to your own personal situation.

This process will be the practical application and implementation of what you have learned in this book put into action in your own life. Let me point out that the phenomenonto become a successful Entrepreneur is possible. By practicing what you have just learned, you will move to the front line in life and with no doubt you are relocating to the top as an eagle in your own area and from today you will not scratch with turkeys.

It is envisaged that you will have an edge over those who do not know or who do not practice the skills presented in this book. If you consistently do the things that other successful people do, nothing in this world will stop you from becoming a great success yourself. You are now the architect of your own destiny. You are behind the steering wheel of your own life.

Entrepreneurship isn't simply about having a great idea. We hear those form all sorts of people all the time. It's rather about implementing these ideas, having the courage to follow-through, often through thick and thin and persevering all the way. As so much goes into the process, I've put together this wide variety of important book to help you along the way.

Lastly, let me conclude by saying whether you have only recently started entertaining the thought of striking out on your own or you've been an entrepreneur for a while, we can all agree on one thing, there is always more to learn. The other thing we can all agree on is that trying to find the information you need to start your own business. Thus why this book is a must read book for you.

References

Books

Aaker, D.A. (2001), Strategic Market Managing, 6th ed. (New Jersey: John Wiley & Sons, Inc)

Aqualiano, N. (2001) Operations Management (New Jersey: McGraw – Hill Companies, Inc)

Bearden, L. (1990), 'Five Imperatives for improving service quality' (Great Brain: Ashford Colour Press)

Boyett, J. and Boyett, J. (1998), The Guru Guide (New Jersey: John Wiley & Sons, Inc)

Buswell, D. (1896), The development of quality measurement system for a UK Bank (London: Phillip Allan Oxford Press)

Blue's Clues for Success: The 8 Secrets Behind a Phenomenal Business by Diane Tracy (Dearborn, 2002).

Chandler, A. (1992) Strategy and Structure (Great Britain: MIT Press)

Charan, R. and Tichy, N. (1999), Every Business is Growth Business: How your Company Can prosper year after year (New Jersey: John Wiley and Sons, Inc)

Chase, R. (2004), Competitive Edge (New Jersey: McGraw – Hill Companies, Inc)

Church, G. (1999), Market Research: Methological Foundation, 7th ed. (London)

Cox, K. and Kotler P. (1998), Marketing Managing and Strategy: 4th ed. (New Jersey: Prentice Hall, Inc)

Cohen, D, and Prusak, L. (2001), "How to Invest in Social Capital" Haward Business Review Volume 79 no. 6 pp 86 – 95

Cole, G.A. (1997) Management Theory and Practice, (Great Britain: Ashford Colour Press, Gosport)

D, Aven R. (2002), "The Empire Strikes Back – Counter Revelatory Strategies for Industry Leaders" Harvard Business Review, Volume 80. no. 11, pp 69 – 79.

Daniels, J. (2004), International Business, (USA: Pearson Educational Limited)

David, F.R. (2001), Strategic Management – Concepts and Cases 8th ed. (New Jersey: Practice Hal, Inc)

Doyley, P. (2002) Marketing Management and Strategy, 3rd ed. (USA: Pearson Education Limited)

Duck, J. (1993:109), Managing Change: The Art of Balancing, Harvard Business Review August

East, R. (1997), Consumer Behaviour: Advances, and Application in Marketing (London: Prentice Hall, Inc)

Ellis, G. (2007), Zero to Million: How to Build a Company to One Million Dollars in Sales (New Jersey: McGraw – Hill Companies, Inc)

Gerson, R. (1994), Measuring Customers Satisfaction (London: Kegan Kegan Limited)

Guerrilla Marketing: Secrets for Making Big Profits from Your Small Businessby Jay Conrad Levinson (Mariner Books, 1998).

Harrigan, K. and Porter, M. (1983), "End – Game Strategies for Declining Industries" Harvard Business Review, July August.

Hisrich, R. (1998) Entrepreneurship, (USA: McGraw – Hill Companies, Inc)

Jeffrey, G. (2001:175), Journal of Business Venture, Harvard Business Review, July

Jones, G. (2005) How to launch and grow the new business, (Great Britain: Bell & Bain Ltd)

Karakaya, F., (2002), "Barriers to Entry in Industrial Markets" Journal of Business and Industrial Marketing, Vol. 17 Issue 5

Lash, L.M. (1920), "Care in service Business" Business and finance Review, pp26 – 30

Laura, M. (1996), Building Adaptive Firm, Small Business Forum (Great Britain: Bell & Bain Lt)

McDonald, M. (1990), Marketing Plans: How to prepare them, How to use them, 4th ed (USA)

McConnell, C.R. and Brue, S.L. (2002). Economics (New Jersey: McGraw – Hill Companies, Inc)

McHugh, M. (2001), Understanding Business, (USA:McGraw – Hill Companies, Inc)

Melkam, A. (1979), How to Handle Major Customers Profitably (USA: Butter - Heinemann)

Nellis, J. (2004), Essence of Business Economics (India: Prentice Hall Private Limited)

Nickles, W. McHugh, J. et al (2005), Understanding Business (New York: McGraw – Hill Companies, Inc)

Oakland, J. (2001), Total Organizational Excellence – Achieving World – Class Performance (USA: Butterworth - Heinemann)

Olson, P. (1993), "Entrepreneurship Start – Up and growth" Business and Finance Review, pp 5 – 20

Own Your Own Corporation: Why the Rich Own Their Own Companies and Everyone Else Works for Them by Garrett Sutton, Robert T.

Pardo, C. (1999), "Key Account Management in Business – to – Business Field: A French Overview" Journal of Business and Industrial Marketing, Vol. 14 Issue 4

Peters, M. (1998), Entrepreneurship, (USA:McGraw – Hill Companies Inc)

Porters, M. (1979), "How Competitive Forces Shape Strategy" Harvard Business Review March – April.

Portraits of Success: 9 Keys to Sustaining Value in Any Business by James Olan Hutcheson (Dearborn, 2002).

Potter, D. (1999), "Success Under Fire: Policies to Prosper in Hostile Time" California Management review, Winter, PP 24 – 38

Radebaugh, L. (2002), International Business, (USA: McGraw Hill Companies, Inc)

Registrar of Companies Data Bank (2008)

Rigby, D. (2002), "Moving Upwards in Downturn" Harvard Business Review Vol. 80 no. 11, pp99-105

Robbins, S.P. (2001), Organizational Behaviour (New Jersey:Prentice Hall, Inc)

Resnblun P. (2003), "Bottom Feeding for Blockbuster Business" Harvard Business Review Volume 81 no. 3, pp52 – 59

OECD (2011), "Public support for business R&D", in OECD, Business Innovation Policies: Selected Country Comparisons, OECD Publishing.

OECD (2010), Why Is Administrative Simplification So Complicated? Looking Beyond 2010, Cutting Red Tape, OECD Publishing.

OECD (2010), SMEs, Entrepreneurship and Innovation, OECD Studies on SMEs and Entrepreneurship, OECD Publishing.

Saunders, M. Lewis P. et al (2000), Research Methods of Business Students, 2nd ed. (Great Britain: Ashford Colour Press Ltd)

Scarborough, M (2003), Effective Small Business, (USA: Pearson Education Limited)

Schumpeter, J. (1996), An Intrinsic Desire to Succeed, (USA: Pearson Education Limited)

Spencer, R. (1999), "Key Accounts: Effectively Managing Strategic Complexity" Journal of Business and Industrial Marketing, Vol 14 Issue 4

Stalk, G. Stern, C (1998), "Perspective on Strategy from the Boston Consulting Group" (USA: John Wiley and Sons, Inc)

Stevenson, W. (2005), Operations Management, (New York: McGraw – Hill Companies, Inc)

Sullivan, D. (2001), International Business, (USA: Pearson Education Limited)

Wilson, D. (1999), Organizational Marketing (New Jersey: International Thosmson Publishing)

World Bank (2013), Doing Business 2013: Smarter Regulations for Small and Medium-Size Enterprises, The World Bank Group, Washington, DC.

Young, E. (1993), "Entrepreneurship's Requisite Areas of Development: A Survey of Top Executives in Successful Entrepreneurial Firm" Journal of Business venture (March 1993)

Zimmer, T. (2000) An Entrepreneurial Approach, (USA: McGraw – Hill Companies, Inc)

Magazines and Newspapers

Black Enterprise <www.blackenterprise.com
Business 2.0 <www.business2.com
Business Startups <www.entrepreneur.com
Business Week <www.businessweek.com
Entrepreneur <www.entrepreneur.com
Fast Company www.fastcompany.com
Forbes <www.forbes.com
www.fortune.com
Franchise Handbook www.franchise1.com
Harvard Business Review <www.harvardbusinessonline.com
Inc. www.inc.com
Red Herring <www.redherring.com
Wall Street Journal<www.wsj.com

Other Web Sites

www.MrAllBiz.com
business.lycos.com
smallbusiness.yahoo.com
www.aarpsmallbiz.com
www.about.com/smallbusiness
www.asbdc-us.org
www.att.sbresources.com
www.bcentral.com
www.bizland.com
www.bloomberg.com
www.business.gov
www.busop1.com
www.chamberbiz.com
www.entreworld.com
www.isquare.com
www.onlinewbc.gov
www.quicken.com/small_business
www.sba.gov
www.score.org
www.usatoday.com/money/smallbusiness/front.htm
www.winwomen.org
www.workz.com